WINNING THE
MARKETING WAR

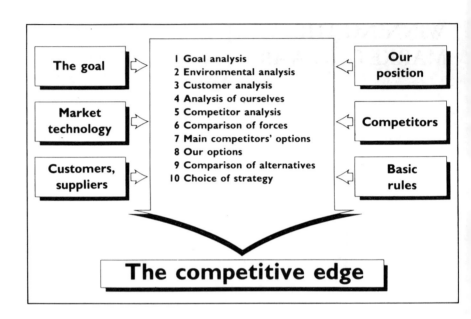

WINNING THE MARKETING WAR

A PRACTICAL GUIDE TO COMPETITIVE ADVANTAGE

by
ROBERT DURO

Marketing Warfare AB, Sweden

Translated from the Swedish by
Tim Crosfield

JOHN WILEY & SONS
Chichester · New York · Brisbane · Toronto · Singapore

Winning the Marketing War, A Practical Guide to Competitive Advantage by Robert Duro.
English language edition, Copyright © 1989 by John Wiley and Sons Ltd.
Originally published in Sweden by Liber Förlag © 1988 by
Robert Duro and Liber Förlag.

Library of Congress Cataloging-in-Publication Data:
Duro, Robert.
     Winning the marketing war : a practical guide to competitive
advantage / Robert Duro.
          p.   cm.
     Bibliography: p.
     ISBN 0 471 92382 6
     1. Marketing—Management.   I. Title.
HF5415.13.D87   1989
658.8—dc20   89-14631
                                                        CIP

British Library Cataloguing in Publication Data:
Duro, Robert
     Winning the marketing war : a practical
     guide to competitive advantage.
     1. Marketing by business firms
     I. Title
     658.8

     ISBN 0 471 92382 6

Typeset by Acorn Bookwork, Salisbury, Wiltshire
Printed and bound in Great Britain by Biddles Ltd, Guildford, Surrey

Contents

Preface

Working out company strategies has traditionally been the prerogative of top management. The strategy handbooks, models and strategy plans they introduce into their companies are often fruits of the relatively uniform management training served up by international business management institutes.

The traditional organization pyramid divides up company responsibilities as follows:

However, today's reality by no means matches this stereotype. What really happens is more like this:

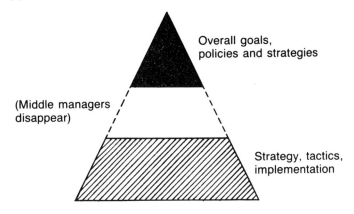

Decisions within a company are being decentralized nearer and nearer to those who work in direct contact with the problems. People work increasingly in teams where strategy, tactics and execution become integrated. The consequence of this is that the numbers involved in the strategy process are growing explosively.

A company *training explosion* is needed now, an explosion in strategic/tactical competitive thinking. We must reckon in terms of training hundreds of people where previously we have been content to send just a few on costly international strategy courses.

At the local level, companies must understand their local conditions of competition, and must adapt Head Office global strategy to these conditions. People have to be able to grasp what is happening on the local market, analyze what is happening there and draw conclusions from it, so they can adopt competition-oriented measures on the local market.

Market information obtained and action taken must be communicated internally and externally at the local level and also to the corporation board so that the formation of company global strategy can be influenced.

The corporation board must commit staff resources for strategic analysis and coordination and must set up staff functions for Business Intelligence.

It surprises me that all this is not self-evident, though it should be. Most decision-makers I have talked to say that they agree with me, but further discussion and their suggestions for action show all too often that they have not really grasped what I mean. Their views on how to adapt to hardening competition are often somewhat bureaucratic.

My central message is not re-expansion of the staff department. What I am telling decision-makers is that they must broaden and deepen the knowledge of strategy within their companies.

This book has been written to meet the real demand companies have for strategic thinking—nobody is supplying this thinking at the moment. By supplementing a reading of the book with a strategy seminar led by an experienced strategy consultant, a company can lay the basis for market operations that have the competitive edge.

The book functions well as a guide on how to create competitive-edge strategies through teamwork and on how to work out tactical moves against competitors.

The case study in Chapters 7 to 10 is based on collaboration with Colonel Kaj Wahlberg, Chief Intelligence Instructor at the Royal Swedish Armed Forces Staff College from 1983 to 1986. Without his collaboration the case study would not have been possible, and I wish to extend my warm thanks to Kaj for his exceptional teaching ability and the brilliant analytical ability which has made description of this 'mini war game' possible.

In the final chapter of the book I have gathered a number of group tasks for you to choose from when formulating your competition strategies in your own company. Choose the tasks that suit you best. Good luck in the marketing war!

Robert Duro

Introduction

The traditional way of viewing company operations as an interplay between the product, the market and the organization is completely inadequate in a world of ever-hardening competition. We have to radically change our ways of looking at our surroundings.

We have to put competition at the center. Competition strategy must direct how we develop our customer strategy, our product strategy and our internal strategy. We must also learn to use external maneuver* to win the necessary freedom of action in our chosen markets.

Today we can plot company operations as in the diagram on page 2.

IBM

With a market share for computers of about 40 percent, IBM is extremely good at competition strategy.

*The meaning of external maneuver is explained in Chapter 2.

IBM sat back and allowed Apple and other computer manufacturers to open up the personal computer market while, with its well-developed intelligence service, it gathered first-class information on markets, products and competition. Then in 1980 an independent IBM unit at Boca Raton, Florida, was given the assignment of developing products for the personal computer market.

In less than a year, IBM introduced its first mass-produced personal computer—the IBM PC. With the launching of its PC family, IBM broke with many of its traditions. The launch went like this:

- The operating system was commissioned from Microsoft, who sold it to all comers
- Externally-produced standard components were used to a large extent
- Peripherals were bought in from other suppliers, but with IBM's logo on the covers
- Independent distributors were the main outlets for the products
- IBM encouraged program manufacturers to develop and sell software.

What happened when such an extremely competition-oriented market leader as IBM used the whole weight of its worldwide organization to introduce a complementary product line was this:

After only two years IBM had 29 percent of the market and had

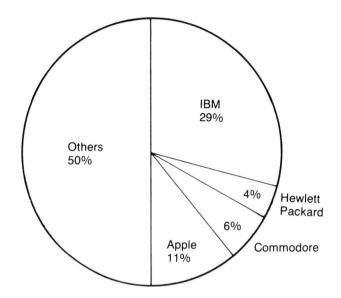

again used its market dominance to dictate data structures and *de facto* standards in the computer industry.

When, after a few years, competition from the numerous IBM copies began to be too troublesome, IBM successively withdrew its open-design policy to make it harder and more expensive for competitors to get around solutions protected by IBM patents.

In this way, competitors were first encouraged to adopt the IBM/Microsoft operating system and then, as soon as the competition started to hurt IBM, were forced to try and get round all the new computer design patents IBM had applied for, to pay licence fees or to put their money into their own computer architecture.

Whatever alternative the competitors chose, IBM had once again achieved an enviable position.

OK

The action of OK, the Swedish oil consumers' cooperative, in 1984–5 is a horror example of poor competition strategy.

OK started operation as an importer of cheap petroleum products from the spot market. With low prices and able use of the advantages its political affiliations afforded, it was able to become market leader in Sweden.

OK's ambitions grew in step with its success: Sweden's largest gas stations with 'do-it-yourself' workshops, its own fleet of tankers, a refinery jointly owned with Texaco and oil prospecting. When the industry was interviewed by the media, it was often OK that spoke in authoritative tones as the self-elected market leader.

When OK started to lose its share of the gasoline market because of the other oil companies' more aggressive promotion and greater price elasticity on the stagnating market, OK ran a big campaign offering its members a 12 öre/liter discount on gas. As OK said, this was to counter the unfair hidden discounts the other oil companies were giving favored groups.

When competitors' gas prices followed down to OK's member's price, OK made further cuts and the battle of prices was on. While competitors were earning from their production of crude oil to compensate for losses in the refinery and distribution sectors, OK was losing in all sectors. After a few weeks of price war and large losses, OK was forced to throw in the sponge, and ran large advertisements promising to remove the special members-only discount. What went wrong?

What OK failed to realize was that lowering the price of gas for a million members meant a frontal attack on the large oil companies. They were forced to join in a general lowering of prices, to save face if for no other reason.

Being the self-elected market leader in Sweden did not help OK when its competitors were Shell, BP, EXXON and Kuwait Oil with their large financial assets and the cheap crude they produced themselves.

THE EXPERIENCE CURVE

Napoleon is supposed to have said that 'God fights on the side of the big battalions.' In the market war, you do not need help from Above to guess correctly at the result of a fight between two competitors if these are of very different sizes and experience.

Assuming that the two companies have comparable distribution systems, products, production apparatuses, organizational efficiency, political and national affiliation, and that they work in the same segment of the market with the same customer groups, then reality looks like this:

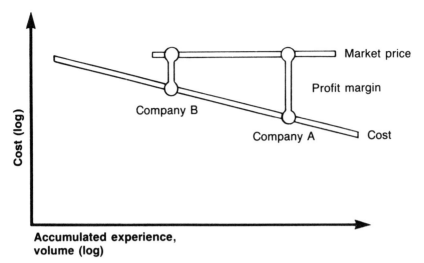

Accumulated experience, volume (log)

In reality, the situation is even more unfavorable for the smaller company since the market leader can often demand a higher sales price because of its better company image and product image.

Japanese companies almost without exception apply the logic of the experience curve. The benign circle, Japanese edition, looks like this:

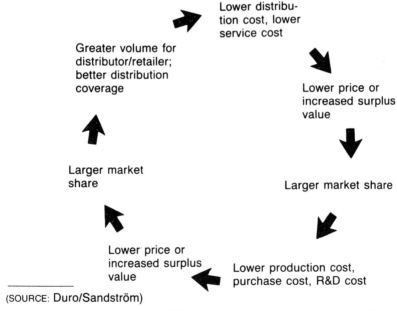

(SOURCE: Duro/Sandström)

Electrolux, Esselte and Swedish Match are companies that apply the same strategy as the Japanese, the 'dominance strategy.' When you risk meeting an opponent you know is working on the benign circle principle, you:

- Try to prevent him from becoming established in your market segment at all.

If this does not work, you:

- Try to prevent him from gathering speed within the benign circle by inhibiting the growth of his market share.

Letting Japanese sub-contractors manufacture products that we have developed at great cost, so that they can build up their purchase and product volumes and learn the product area at the same time, is something many companies have later bitterly regretted.

If we cannot manage to arrest a competitor's progress in the benign circle and realize we are going to be outfought in the long run, we must firmly diversify parts of our total market operation or choose a market segment where we will not meet that competitor.

It is vital in the market war to form a correct appreciation of one's strengths compared to those of one's competitors. Trying to beat a competitor who is significantly stronger than oneself in the same market segment, processing the same customers with the same offers, is poor competition strategy.

We will win against a superior opponent only by refusing to fight on his terms, choosing instead the terrain and the methods of combat that favor us and put the opponent at a disadvantage.

THE SPENDRUP SAGA

A ban on class II (medium-strength) beer in 1977 and the consequent drop in beer sales had drastic consequences for the Swedish brewing trade. Breweries went bankrupt or were bought up one after the other by the big, state-owned Pripps Breweries, and closed down.

Grängesberg Breweries (now Spendrup) were also badly hit, and they struggled with the threat of liquidation over them.

An assessment of the strength relationships between Pripps and Spendrup at the end of the 1970s would look roughly as in the table on the opposite page, from Pripps' angle:

Looking at the most important success factors within brewing, we see that Spendrup was thus hopelessly inferior to Pripps, the market leader. Apart from liquidation, Spendrup had basically two alternatives.

Geographical area: Sweden

Market: Beer

Market success factors	Pripps' strength relative to Spendrup's						
	Weaker			Equal			Stronger
	1	2	3	4	5	6	7
1 Distribution efficiency							
2 Production efficiency							
3 Marketing efficiency							
4 Service-mindedness							
5 Range							
6 Image, quality, packaging							

Option 1

Spendrup could try to improve its cost position *vis-à-vis* Pripps and from its geographical base north of Stockholm attack Pripps in the Stockholm area with the same price level, or in fact a lower price level, since the market leader is often the price leader.

This strategy—I call it the *direct strategy*—can in this case be likened to attacking a well-barricaded opponent at the spot where his fortress walls are thickest and his cannons largest.

Option 2

Spendrup's alternative was to attack Pripps where Pripps could not exploit its enormous size. Note that Spendrup was only one-thirteenth the size of Pripps in 1977.

Spendrup therefore had to try and find holes in the Pripps fortress or force Pripps to fight the market war outside the castle walls on terrain carefully chosen by Spendrup. I call this second strategy the *indirect strategy*.

Spendrup elected to fight Pripps using option 2: the indirect strategy.

In a competition situation such as the one Pripps was faced with in 1977, skill is not enough: an element of luck is also needed. Spendrup had just that. Löwenbrau Breweries tried to persuade Pripps to brew Löwenbrau beer on license, but Pripps must have thought that it was enough with Tuborg and Carlsberg. Löwenbrau then signed up Spendrup instead.

What Spendrup achieved through the license agreement was this:

- Full use of its brewing capacity
- Better knowledge of how to brew a quality beer
- Knowledge of how to market a quality beer
- Access to the State Liquor Monopoly's distribution apparatus, since the first license product was class III – strong beer

- Good liquidity since by law the tax on strong beer was paid some months after Spendrup had been paid by the Liquor Monopoly.

Had not Spendrup started its collaboration with Löwenbrau with an established strong beer, a sound built-in distribution economy and liquidity, the Spendrup saga would most likely have ended here.

However, now Spendrup acquired the economic resources for investing in a product the market was crying out for—a popular beer that tasted like the withdrawn medium beer—*a premium folk beer*.

Spendrup's launch strategy

1. New Folk Beer—Quality Beer   To fight Pripps with a regular folk beer would never work. The only chance was to use the know-how gained from collaboration with Löwenbrau to make a premium folk beer.

Luck played its part here too, since Pripps also had premium folk beers through the Tuborg and Carlsberg agencies, but the company did not invest actively in marketing what fantastic beers it brewed under license.

This was probably because of the well-known 'not invented here' syndrome—plus the fact that it naturally pays better to sell one's own beer rather than a license product if customers do not care what beer they drink. Pripps' inability to market 'quality' in its own beers or in license beers played into Spendrup's hands.

2. New name   Grängesberg does not sound like a good beer, but Spendrup sounds Danish. Everybody knows that the Danes are good at brewing good beer, so why not use the Spendrup family name for the new premium beer? This is just what the Spendrup brothers did.

3. New packaging   In 1977 folk beer (the weakest and lowest-taxed class in Sweden) was sold in cans and strong beer in bottles—everybody knew that too. Champagne bottles are associated with pretty labels—that is also a well-known fact. So when Spendrup bottled their premium folk beer in bottles with champagne-like labels, people realized that it must be something quite out of the ordinary.

Spendrup had grasped the fact that quality *must be attractively packed*, otherwise nobody believes that you are selling a quality product.

4. *High price* A quality product must be more expensive, otherwise people tend to doubt that it is quality they are buying. So Spendrup was dearer than Pripps, of course.

5. *Stepwise market penetration* Spendrup decided to launch its folk beer a step at a time. For one thing, the company had insufficient production capacity, and for another, it wanted to read off how the offer was being received target group by target group. Timewise, the launch was like this:

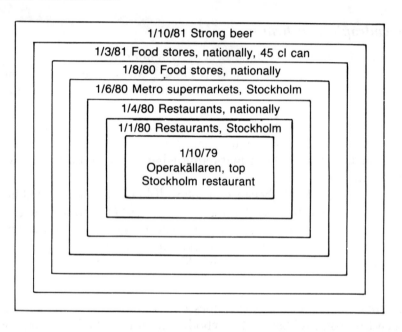

Spendrup enlarges its bridgehead

Now that Spendrup through its flank attack had established itself as a quality manufacturer, the bridgehead was successfully enlarged through the introduction of different premium products: Spendrup Light Ale, Spendrup Bavarian folk beer, Spendrup strong beer, the Pepsi Cola agency and the minerals agency for the well-known quality brand Canada Dry.

The crowning glory was when Spendrup managed to get the super-premium strong beer Old Gold into the State Liquor Monopoly, even though it was way down on the waiting list. The lauching of Old Gold followed the same basic principle as the introduction of

Spendrup's folk beer, the so-called Cafe Opera principle: 'If it's hard to get in, getting in's interesting.'

Spendrup used the same ploy on the restaurants and the public, and this pressurized restaurants and the Liquor Monopoly into including Old Gold in their selections. Old Gold rapidly became a big Spendrup seller.

THE GENERAL FORMULA FOR STRATEGY

Spendrup's brilliant marketing operation can be illustrated with French general André Beaufre's formula for strategic operations.

THE GENERAL FORMULA FOR STRATEGY

$$S = uMPT$$

where

u = the unique factor in any situation
M = Material deployment of forces
P = Psychological forces
T = the time factor

Spendrup made use of the unique factor u:

- It realized that people were tired of watery folk beer and wanted a good beer instead—a premium folk beer
- It cashed in on the renaissance of individualism. Drinking Spendrup's premium beer was a way of showing that one did not follow the crowd: one did not drink beer from the state-owned market leader Pripps
- The current state inquiry into the brewing industry ('Brewinvest') was a godsend for Spendrup, for it came up with what was in effect an easily attackable suggestion for a monopoly. By referring in the media to the 'Brewinvest' inquiry, Spendrup could point to the risks of Pripps' inflated market dominance, which was reaching monopoly proportions within the industry.

Spendrup was hopelessly inferior to Pripps in material resources (M). Spendrup compensated for this by:

- Using the State Liquor Monopoly national distribution

apparatus for the Spendrup strong beer range to restaurants and liquor shops

- Acquiring independent forwarding agents who sold Spendrup products on a commission basis
- Having grocery wholesalers take care of distribution to retail outlets
- Concentrating sales to the Stockholm area
- Manufacturing known 'brand products' under license to avoid development costs and to lower marketing costs.

Spendrups used the psychological factor (*P*) by:

- Offering good service to the customer, and at the same time a purchasing alternative to Pripps. Customers could now lean on Pripps with the 'or else' they would raise their Spendrup orders. 'If you've got a Spendrup crate in the shop, you'll get a better deal from Pripps' was a message that must have got through to the dealers
- Showing itself to the media as the small, select family brewery (David) battling with the big bad state brewery, Pripps (Goliath). Everybody loves an underdog
- Taking advantage of the internal management-versus-union power struggle going on at Pripps and of Pripps' clumsy market operation. Psychological strength is relative. Spendrup became stronger as Pripps became weaker.

Lastly, Spendrup used the time factor (*T*) through:

- Its stepwise market penetration, which meant that it did not overextend its resources in terms of time
- Concentration on quality products with resulting high prices. This rapidly created the good profitability and liquidity needed on account of Spendrup's weak financial starting position
- Its success in interesting important customers such as the ICA and Metro food chains in taking up Spendrup shares when the company went public on the OTC list. Being introduced on the Stock Exchange gave Spendrup access to the necessary capital for investment in modern production plant and distribution apparatus. This was a must for matching up to Pripps in the long run.

THE CRUCIAL IMPORTANCE OF PSYCHOLOGY

Strategists of the market war do not, alas, always realize that strategic interplay is a psychological interplay of wills. You have to get your opponent (competitor, customer, supplier, whatever) where you want him, get him to accept your own solution.

Spendrup was successful in the strategic/tactical operation against Pripps because its generals knew—and Pripps' didn't—how to exploit psychological market forces. Spendrup managed above all to enlist media support in the psychological battle for the beer-drinker's approval.

Geographical area: Stockholm

Market: Restaurants—Premium Beer

Market success factors	Pripps' strength relative to Spendrup's						
	Weaker			Equal			Stronger
	1	2	3	4	5	6	7
1 Image, quality, packaging	▬						
2 Service-mindedness	▬▬						
3 Marketing efficiency	▬▬▬						
4 Range	▬▬▬▬▬▬						
5 Distribution efficiency	▬▬▬▬▬▬						
6 Production efficiency	▬▬▬▬						

We can see from the diagram that Spendrup initially chose to stress (total) quality, packaging and image, all success factors that leave the way open for affecting the market psychologically.

In the following chapters I shall examine how to form a strategy plan for the competitive edge. Here, the importance of psychology in the marketing war is an ever-present theme.

In our work together at Marketing Warfare AB, Björn Sandström and I chose the name BATTLE for the model of strategy I shall now present.

BATTLE is our adaptation of the internationally recognized military appreciation model for how to beat the 'enemy.' It is thus extremely well suited for creating competitive-edge strategy plans for hardening competition situations.

The BATTLE model in its latest modified form looks like this:

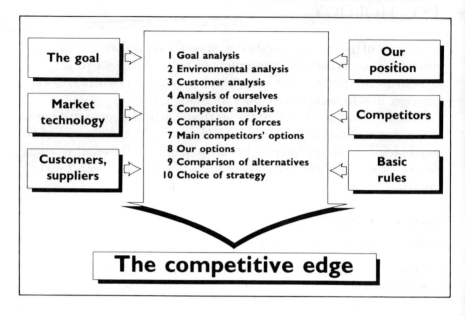

1 Goal analysis

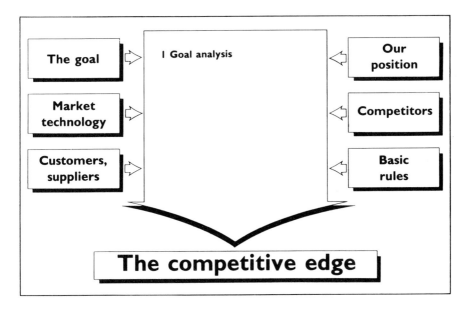

For a company to realize its full potential, three things are needed:

- *Fundamental values* that serve to guide how members of the company are to work and act, both within the company and towards the rest of the world. These values must permeate the whole organization
- *An explicit business idea* that will tell everybody working in the company what business they are in
- *Realistic goals* at strategic level, broken down into sub-goals for practical use at different levels. The overall goal and individuals' own work goals must be clearly stated, and everyone must understand why the goal is what it is.

15

FUNDAMENTAL VALUES

In his book, *The IBM Way*, Buck Rodgers (Vice-President, Marketing at IBM for ten years) writes that the chief reason for IBM's fantastic success lies in the fundamental values that IBM's founder Thomas J. Watson, Senior, formulated in 1914:

(1) The individual must be respected.
(2) The customer must be given the best possible service.
(3) Excellence and superior performance must be pursued.

If these principles really are the chief reason for IBM's success, then it ought to be easy as pie for competitors to formulate something along the same lines and then become as successful as IBM. However, unfortunately the truth is not that simple.

IBM

What sets IBM apart from most companies is the practical steps taken to ensure that people live up to these principles. This is what IBM does:

The individual must be respected

During his time as an NCR salesman Thomas J. Watson, Senior, experienced selling as a low-prestige job. This he wanted to change. So at IBM salesmen are treated as company heroes. Everybody knows that the sales staff are the corporation's VIPs, and since at IBM everybody sells in some way or another, anyone who performs well at selling comes in for this treatment.

Good work performance gives dividends in the form of bonuses and other notice in the form of diplomas, membership of the 'One Hundred Percent Club,' membership of the 'Gold Club,' incentive trips or a dinner for two at a high-class restaurant. The other side of the coin is that IBM is just as quick to correct poor achievement as to reward excellence.

IBM works very actively to create a small-company atmosphere in the corporation. One way is to keep down the size of the group and the numbers of staff who report to one chief.

IBM follows the principle of lifetime appointment, which requires people to be prepared to change their work assignments from time to time. Job rotation has long been practiced at IBM. For a time, this went so far that people said IBM was short for 'I've been moved'.

IBM policy is to recruit internally. This gives people who work hard and wish to advance in the corporation greater chances of doing so.

The open-door policy at IBM means that individuals can take grudges all the way up the hierarchy to the IBM president in Armonk, USA.

IBM runs Annual Performance Appraisals, at which the individual and his superior check out how work assignments have been handled during the year. They also consider the next year's objectives: what demands these will place on the individual and how they may affect his salary position.

The 'Executive Interview' gives the individual the opportunity to meet the next higher manager over his own for a free exchange of ideas. This enables higher managers to learn more about the individual's achievement, but also provides chances for the individual to ask questions about the corporation.

Then we come to those small but important details: no reserved parking places, managers eat together with other employees, no titles on doors, landscape offices preferably, for ease of communication, and so on.

The customer must be given the best possible service

Right from the appointment interview, the appointee is made to realize that the customer comes first, and that IBM has clear rules for how customers are to be treated. If the appointee cannot accept the rules, then he/she had better not work for IBM.

At IBM, everybody is a salesperson. Every job description states clearly how the individual's job contributes to the maintenance of good customer relations and selling. Upper management in all functions within the corporation are allocated a number of customers with whom they, together with the salespeople, have to maintain continuous contact.

The way IBM works, the salespeople become specialists in different areas, for example finance, insurance, etc. They share their specialist knowledge with their customers through conferences, reports, visits to IBM's specialist departments and visits with customers who have the answers to similar problems.

In this way, IBM functions as something of an *in-house consultant* for its customers. This adds to the 'sense of security' which could be the chief reason why the customer buys IBM.

Staff training is important at IBM. An IBM salesperson, for

example, is reckoned to spend 15 percent of his/her time being trained. However, customer training is also important, so that customers will buy more. Accordingly, they are invited regularly to attend various IBM training courses.

In short, IBM tries to establish a relationship where the customer and IBM are partners. It was not by accident that Buck Rodgers said that the greatest compliment a customer could pay him was to observe, of an IBM salesman, 'I'm not sure if he's working for me or for you.'

From the customer's angle, we may wonder if this is always such a good thing: what kind of negotiating position versus IBM does the customer have if the collaboration is so close that he does not know if a person is working for IBM or for him?

Excellence and superior performance must be pursued

The goal is perfection—zero defects—both in products and in the service IBM gives customers. Great care is taken to see that the people who are hired fit in with the IBM work ethic. This lays the foundation. Employee performance is followed up continually, and the employee gets quick feedback on how IBM thinks he has done. In this way, everybody learns in concrete terms what IBM means by perfection.

Through the internal recruitment policy and job development programs (The Executive Resources Program) those employees advance who IBM thinks best meet the demand for perfection.

Three-monthly interviews with sales people and systems analysts show whether they think IBM is doing a good job of marketing. Other personnel categories are also interviewed regarding their views on internal and external issues. The picture is completed through regular interviews with customers to find out what they think of IBM.

IBM is sometimes branded as an iron fist in a velvet glove. A look at the corporation's routines for inquiring into the reasons for losing a customer shows that this picture is not altogether incorrect.

If a customer cancels an order or returns IBM equipment, IBM requires that the commission be returned not from the salesman who sold the equipment, but from the person currently responsible for the customer contact. This, says Buck Rodgers, is to ram home the important lesson that the salesperson must really care about the customer even when there are no orders directly in the pipeline.

Profit and loss reports are compiled every month to show in detail why IBM won or lost a deal. Numerous copies of these are distributed

18

to managers throughout the organizational hierarchy. This is not head-hunting, says Rodgers, but a way of correcting the mistakes that led to the loss of the order.

Some concluding comments: reading Buck Rodgers' description of how IBM works gives the impression of a successful, hard-working, well-disciplined, even military, organization, but one with, perhaps, too much of the iron fist and the superman ideal. Copying IBM at every point therefore seems not altogether desirable.

However, don't throw out the baby with the bath water. An important condition for success is to do as IBM does: formulate and communicate basic company values and see that people live up to them in their daily work.

(MAIN SOURCE: *The IBM Way*, Buck Rodgers, Harper and Row. OTHER SOURCES: *IBM—Colossus in Transition*, Robert Sobel, Times Books; IBM employees past and present; IBM distributors' reports on IBM)

A CLEAR BUSINESS IDEA

It is essential for employees to understand what business the company is in. A company with different areas of business requires several business ideas. Within the different areas, too, it may help to combine the idea with somewhat more concrete guidelines for the sub-units.

Bergman and Beving

One of Sweden's most successful companies is Bergman and Beving. The company was founded 80 years ago with the following business idea: 'As general agent to market high-technology products to technology-based enterprises and institutions'.

The group now comprises 40 independent result units working within four areas:

- Computers/electronics
- Energy
- Medical technology/chemistry/biochemistry
- Dental/precious metals.

What is needed in the Bergman and Beving case is for the overall business idea to be complemented with somewhat more concrete definitions for the different companies.

Let us start from the bottom defining what business we are in. There are different ways of doing this:

Product-oriented or market-oriented definitions*

Type of company	Product-oriented definition	Market-oriented definition
Revlon	We sell cosmetics	We sell hope
Railroad	We run railroad traffic	We are a transportation company
Movie company	We make movies	We are in the entertainment business
Shell	We sell petroleum products	We supply energy

*See the article by Theodore Levitt, Marketing Myopia, *Harvard Business Review*, July–August 1960.

It is important to pause fairly often and ask ourselves whether the overall business definition is correct. From the competition angle, a product-oriented business definition may be the correct alternative as an overall guide; but a market-oriented definition is best in most cases.

Irrespective of the company level for which the business idea is formulated, I consider the following questions should be thought through before the formula is committed to paper:

(1) What are your markets? Who are your customers?
(2) What customer need do you satisfy?
(3) What do you have to offer?
(4) Why should the customer choose just you? What is unique and/or superior about your offer to a customer?

Marketing Warfare's business idea is like this: 'We supply the company's need of competitive-edge market operations by offering in-depth and in-breadth competition-oriented training and supportive consultancy.'

This business idea answers the first three questions, but not what is unique and competitively superior. This question we answer when we describe, to a potential customer, what our business idea would mean for him in concrete terms, for it is in concrete market action that one shows one's competitive edge.

Hard Rock Cafe

The Hard Rock Cafe (HRC) in Stockholm belongs to a very successful international chain with restaurants in London (1977), New York (1984), Dallas (1986), Tokyo (1987) and Reykjavik (1987). The Stockholm restaurant is run as a franchise by Stock Rock AB, a Swedish company with some 400 shareholders. 1987 turnover was about 35 million SEK and the number of employees was about 75.

In the summer of 1986, the board and the restaurant management engaged a consultant who together with them was to work out a strategic plan for the operation.

The background was this. In the autumn of 1983, two private individuals acquired rights to run HRC restaurants in Sweden plus options for Denmark, Finland and Norway. The then very successful investment company Skrinet undertook, through a consortium, to supply capital for projecting and opening the first unit.

When the HRC opened on April 16, 1985 to the sounding of brass and the clashing of cymbals, the project had been delayed by over six months. During that time, investment costs had grown and the bill finally came to some 25 to 30 million SEK—nearly double the original estimates.

There was wide disagreement among the owners as to how the Stockholm HRC should be run, and this led to mismanagement. Just before the opening, the Executive Vice-President left following suspicions of irregularities. Yet the public had been waiting expectantly to learn what was so special about Sweden's most widely publicized restaurant launch. The HRC was already a success even before it opened.

A TV report team were there to immortalize the happening when the ribbon was cut, so that all Sweden could follow the inauguration the same evening. For the first few weeks, there were continual queues outside.

However, the party was quickly over. Quite soon there appeared negative articles by disappointed journalists writing of 'Sweden's most expensive hamburger,' of 'earsplitting rock music that rules out all conversation' and of 'Hard Rock to crash?'

In a few months the shares slumped to a third of their issue price. The original owners in the consortium around Skrinet sold their shares in the company and pulled out. The franchiser, tired of all the hassle, simply cancelled the franchise agreement. Sales continued to dwindle, month after month and, at the worst point, the negative result was nearly as large as the turnover.

From this point Anders Johansson, Executive Vice-President from November 1985, had with the help of his middle management and with enormous effort succeeded in breaking the downward trend so that when work was started on the strategy plan in the summer of 1986, a faint upswing could be discerned.

However, the impression of a flop remained. If the consultant asked friends what they knew about the Hard Rock Cafe he nearly always got depressing answers:

- Are they still open? I thought they'd gone bust
- Surely they've closed down. You sure they're still in business?
- Sweden's most expensive hamburger. Earsplitting music.

At the first meeting, someone mentioned that the HRC should serve today's special at meal ticket prices, and suggested meatballs and jam, pancakes and peas and other traditional Swedish dishes.

So the consultant asked the members of the seminar if the Hard Rock Cafe was a Swedish home cooking restaurant, a pizzeria, maybe even a Chinese restaurant. 'No! No! No!' they cried. 'Okay, but just what are you then?' The answer came back . . . 'The Hard Rock Cafe is *Stockholm's Real American Restaurant and Rock'n'Roll Museum.*'

'Sure, and you're thinking of serving Swedish home cooking,' the consultant countered. 'The Hard Rock Cafe is a unique restaurant. It's the best of America of the nineteen-fifties, and at the same time a rock fans' shrine.'

In the same way as IBM imprints its basic values, work was started to consciously formulate what was meant by: 'THE REAL AMERICAN RESTAURANT.'

The HRC is an American concept of food and service, a unique milieu, a Rock'n'Roll museum with background music from the 1950s to the present. All HRC restaurants follow the same principles, with some adaptation to local conditions. When the Stockholm HRC opened, the then management thought a number of changes in the business ideas would be necessary to suit Swedish guests. The new management, however, thought that the original concept should be brought out, and had already started promoting it to the public.

A number of strategy seminars became the key to how the message should be got over. The members did not start from the beginning:

much had already been done and written down, but a collective sense of purpose was lacking.

The practically minded will wonder what the HRC served as today's special. American home cooking of course—what else?

I return to the HRC at several places in the book since, in view of its size and activity, it is a very useful example of how a company downswing can be turned with a thought-out strategy.

REALISTIC GOALS

At the start of the 1980s the then President of IBM, John Opel, established the corporation's overall objectives for the rest of the 1980s to maintain its position as market leader:*

(1) To grow with the industry, not only in traditional areas such as mainline computers but also in newer areas.
(2) To exhibit leadership both in the development and production of high-quality, reliable products and in sales and service.
(3) To be *the* most efficient and effective in everything it does—*the* low-cost producer, *the* low-cost seller, *the* low-cost servicer and *the* low-cost administrator.
(4) To sustain profitability, which funds the growth of the business.

Some goals! Nobody who knows how conscientiously IBM applies its basic values need doubt for a second that the corporation's overall objective for the 1980s is broken down into detailed operative goals which are carefully followed up.

Bergman and Beving†

The Bergman and Beving Group is run according to two profitability objectives.

Return on own capital

Good profitability is a prerequisite for expansion and growth. The group's long-term profitability objective is to achieve a yield of at least 25 percent on average own capital. During 1986–7, however, we did not quite reach this goal, the result being 24.1 percent.

*SOURCE: *The IBM Way*, Buck Rodgers, Harper and Row.
†SOURCE: Extract from Bergman and Beving's Annual Report 1986–7.

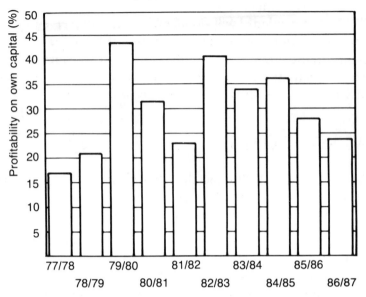

Yield on own capital

Profitability R/RK

For internal assessments of profitability, we use the measure R/RK:

R = Result before tax
RK = Tied-up working capital (stock plus receivables minus amounts due to suppliers)

The R/RK measure of profitability is suitable for a commercial business where there is no need for heavy investment in production plant.
It affords, among other things, the following advantages:

- Profitability R/RK can be measured down to the product level
- Every member of the company can budget to affect his/her R/RK.

Our business philosophy has the aim that an established business idea should give at least 45 per cent R/RK. This means that an annual expansion of about 15 percent can be self-financing.
For the group as a whole, the 45 percent objective has been exceeded for the past five years. During 1986–7 we reached 68 percent R/RK.

It often happens when people are drawing up a strategy plan that the

24

plan develops in such a way that we all feel a certain course of action is self-evident. It is *common sense*.

However, then come the doubts—will the customer really do what has been agreed on? The state the Hard Rock Cafe had got into is probably not so unusual. The HRC did not want for a goal—but they did lack collective awareness of what their goals were and efficient ways of reaching them.

Hard Rock Cafe

At the first seminar the Hard Rock Cafe's operational goals were discussed, what exactly was meant by the different goals and why each was as it was. In note form, the following goals were formulated.

(1) *Food*
   Top-quality foodstuffs
   Large (American) and tasty helpings
   Value for money (the opposite of 'Sweden's most expensive hamburger')
(2) *Music*
   Rock music from the 1950s on, varied to suit the public and the time of day
(3) *Milieu*
   Arena-like layout; guests can see each other
   Very special decor—a Rock'n'Roll museum
   The atmosphere (positive American—something must be happening all the time)
(4) *Service*
   Quick and friendly
   Considerate
   Choice of how food is prepared
(5) *Staff*
   Highly motivated staff
   Well-turned-out staff
   Regulation dress

The financial goals formulated looked like this:

(1) Yield: x% of own capital   1987
              y% of own capital   1988

(2) Turnover: x crowns per month 1987
              y crowns per month 1988

(3) Material costs:	$x\%$ of sales	1987
	$y\%$ of sales	1988
(4) Payroll:	$x\%$ of sales	1987
	$y\%$ of sales	1988

Now everyone knew where they were, and all could deliberately get down to making the HRC rise Phoenix-like from its own ashes and climb to the stars.

Every company, then, should ensure that it formulates:

(1) Basic values.
(2) A clear business idea.
(3) Realistic goals.

These must not be empty cliches, but are the expression of the organization's collective awareness. The greater the number of staff members involved in the process the greater the chance of success.

Thus goals and strategies should be the results of teamwork at company level, adapted to local market conditions by local teams.

2 Environmental analysis

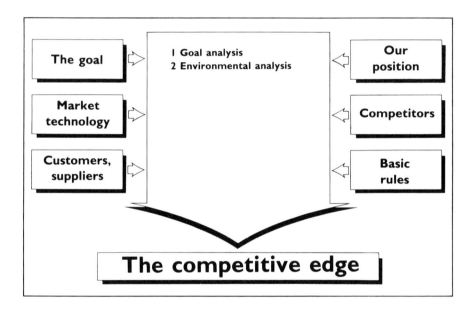

The competitive edge

EXTERNAL MANEUVER

In the market war it is essential to gain maximal freedom of action. Paradoxically enough, this is done through action outside the market in which one is operating. Freedom of action is ensured 'globally' even if the war is a local one.

It is largely a matter of psychological maneuvering, of trying to make different moves serve the same ends—political and economic. External maneuver usually contains some of the following elements:

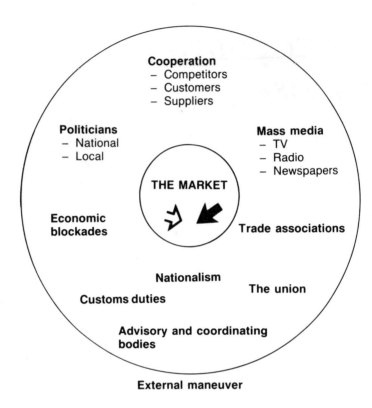

External maneuver

IBM

IBM is extremely skilful at adapting to different national and cultural demands.

At the beginning of the 1980s, IBM wished to start manufacturing personal computers in Mexico. The corporation wanted to own the plant 100 percent, but the Mexican government wanted at least 51 percent—which is usual in developing countries. To obtain permission to start production, IBM increased its investment fourteenfold, promised to export 90 percent of the computers manufactured and also promised further investment outside the personal computer area.

Over and above this, IBM also promised support to seven Mexican universities, which would give the corporation a long-term edge, since being in on the development of a country's university system is no bad merit.

In a lecture on strategy delivered at the beginning of the 1980s, the Executive Vice-President of IBM in Sweden, Carl Hugo Bluhme, reported how the Järfälla plant was trying to increase the numbers of components bought from Norway so as to achieve a better balance between the export and import of IBM products to and from Norway.

IBM early realized the forces that could be turned against it if the corporation did not actively spread its manufacturing to the different countries that buy its products and if it did not adapt its operations locally to national cultures.*

Ericsson

Poor growth and high R&D costs caused Ericsson to sign a number of strategic cooperation agreements in quick succession during 1987:

- An initial cooperation agreement with Digital concerns bank terminals, and there is an explicit ambition to extend the cooperation to other areas of Ericsson Information Systems operations
- An agreement has been signed with IBM to integrate telephone technology (AXE) and computer technology in public networks. The agreement makes it possible for the telecommunications agencies themselves to create programs for new integrated telephone services, to be run on the IBM mainframe computers they most commonly have.

  If Ericsson's Public Telecommunications unit and IBM manage to establish joint programming standards, this will put them in a strong position relative to the world's telephone administrations
- An agreement with Texas Instruments in the field of microelectronics relieves Ericsson Components of development costs
- With Siemens and the French Matra, there is a cooperation agreement regarding a future European automobile telephone system.

These different cooperation agreements could only be the beginning, since Ericsson realizes that, with continually increasing development and promotion costs, and also for political reasons, it can no longer manage the role of high-tech lone wolf on world markets.

---

*Contains information taken from an article by Åke Gidlund in *The World of IBM*, published by CW-production.

Hard Rock Cafe

It was necessary to clean up the tarnished image resulting from the negative write-ups in the press. There was only one way of doing this: successive improvements in quality, service and cleanliness.

Unfortunately, measures of this type take a long time to show the desired effect. Management therefore needed to find other, parallel, measures to speed up the flow of guests. They decided to concentrate their efforts on two main activities: dance and live music.

In the restaurant trade, good relations with the authorities are essential, since it is they who decide on licensing and opening times. Before opening, the HRC had been granted a liquor license until 1.00 a.m. No dance license had been applied for. Because of the competition, however, the HRC needed to remain open until 3.00 a.m. and to have dancing on certain days—Wednesdays, Fridays and Saturdays. The authorities were against this because some functions in the Stock Rock Rooms (HRC's suite for private parties) had disturbed residents in the building.

The restaurant itself had been soundproofed for millions of crowns when it was being fitted out. All functions in the Stock Rock Rooms that could disturb residents were vetoed. Residents in the building were invited to a meeting at which they were informed of the new management's policy. HRC's management also worked actively to ensure that guests did not cause disturbance when entering or leaving the HRC. After more than a year of discussion with the relevant authorities, a liquor license and a dance license until 2 a.m. were granted provisionally.

Management worked to have the company considered as a serious one. However, just being a serious company was not enough—the HRC had to blazon it out. As many people associate a rock joint with violence, the HRC sponsored 'The Non-Fighting Generation' with various activities to demonstrate the values it stood for.

The HRC was to be Rock'n'Roll at its best. The whole range was to be represented, from the 1950s to the latest hits. To underscore the importance of music at the HRC, a person was hired solely for booking and promoting live bands.

Also important was the promotion of personal contacts with record companies, music journalists, local and national radio, TV entertainment producers and well-known entertainment journalists for their cooperation and good press coverage. This was a lot more difficult than management thought. Many contacts had been badly handled during the time before opening. Interest grew, however, as the market realized that the HRC was really going in for music. Well-known bands attracted even people who were most negative, and more than 200 live bands played at the HRC in 1986–7.

MARKET SEGMENTATION

The idea behind market segmentation is to divide the market into different areas. Concentrating forces, one gains the competitive edge locally in chosen areas. A company can exploit its strengths and avoid being hampered by its weaknesses. Resources can be concentrated within different company functions so as to achieve competitive advantages.

Hard Rock Cafe

HARD ROCK CAFE
—Love all serve all

This was the starting slogan when the HRC's operation was segmented. The HRC loves all and serves all but—note—not at the same time! Love remains but its object changes, as the poet said. Here are the Hard Rock Cafe market segments:

Segment	Weekly times
1 Rock band evening	Tuesday evenings
2 Evenings out	Wednesdays, Fridays and Saturdays
3 Sunday brunch	Sundays, 11.00 a.m.–5.00 p.m.
4 Family rock	Saturdays, 11.00 a.m.–6.00 p.m.
5 Dinner guests	Mondays, Wednesdays–Sundays, 6.00–10.00 p.m.
6 Business lunches	Mondays–Fridays, 11.00 a.m.– 2.30 p.m.
7 Today's lunch menu	Mondays–Fridays, 11.00 a.m.– 2.30 p.m.
8 Tourists	Daily until about 10.00 p.m.

This was a natural segmentation since customers had such varying

31

needs during a week. Let us examine customer needs for three of the segments:

1. Rock band evening—Tuesdays

- Good rock bands
- Atmosphere (restaurant and public)
- To be seen and to meet friends
- Beer and light meals (smaller than the regular HRC jumbo portions).

Goals for the live operations were defined as: good rock bands to attract more guests, chiefly those who had never set foot in the HRC because they had heard the negative rumors. There would therefore be a mix of bands, all within Rock'n'Roll of course, to satisfy as many tastes as possible.

The HRC also took great pains over sound and lighting for each performance, to enhance the atmosphere. Groups and their crews were to be well looked after by HRC staff, so that they could recommend the HRC to other groups.

Last but not least fees for the groups were to be covered by the evening's takings.

With these goals in mind, the new band-booker began the rounds of Swedish and overseas agents.

Bills announcing the program for the month were distributed and put up all over town. The newspapers started writing about the performers, but were still critical of the HRC: 'A brilliant concert, but what miserable premises, what expensive, dry hamburgers.' After four months, the critics had fallen silent and the HRC was leader in live music.

4. Family Rock—Saturdays, 11.00 a.m.–6.00 p.m.

- Cheap, value-for-money food and drink
- Entertainment for the children
- Presents for the children, e.g. balloons and bags of goodies
- Atmosphere (restaurant and public)
- Parents' clear conscience.

The main goal was to attract the whole family. Once the children had visited the HRC, we believed, they would give their parents no peace until they promised to take them again. In this way it would be possible to build a group of regular customers consisting of children. The HRC did everything to give the children a good time. For the first Saturdays, ads were run in the daily press. Magicians, jugglers and clowns appeared, balloons filled the restaurant and every child received a bag of goodies with a Hard Rock sign.

The kids loved it! And the parents?—They found it a little untidy, the hamburgers rather dear and the sound level rather high, but they all agreed 'the children like it here, so we'll definitely come again.' Family Rock quickly became the best selling period in the week.

8. Tourists—Daily until about 10.00 p.m.

- Hard Rock Cafe merchandise
- Good image
- Rock'n'Roll museum decor
- Quality food
- American food.

In the spring of 1987 steps were taken to help tourists discover that Stockholm had a Hard Rock Cafe. Together with an advertising agency, the idea of a simple tourist map, the 'Hard Rock Map,' was hatched, with ten specially trained 'Hard Rock Ambassadors' whose main job was to distribute it to selected hotels and tourist attractions and to approach strolling tourists directly.

The response was way above expectations! Sales of merchandise tripled, and on the best day reached 60,000 crowns (mainly T-shirts and sweatshirts).

Alfa Laval

In a lecture on strategy in the early 1980s, Executive Vice-President Harry Faulkner showed the following illustrative picture of two market segments at Alfa Laval:

	Large marine separators	Small marine separators
Vessel size	>2000 Dwt	<2000 Dwt
Customer	Shipyards	Shipyards
Decision-maker	Ship owner	Shipyards
Geographical sales area	The world	Regional
Value of worldwide service	Large	Small
Main competitor	WF/MKK	MKK
Market growth 1980–85	1%	8%

This segmentation gives the answer to why Alfa Laval was so violently attacked by the Japanese in smaller marine separators.

- For the smaller marine separators, the final customer and the decision-maker are one and the same, which means fewer customer visits and simpler customer processing. The Japanese were able to build up their sales and service organization successively without drawbacks
- They gained the advantage of working in a growth market with considerably larger volumes to handle than the market for large marine separators could offer.

Alfa Laval's strategy was thus to try and stop the Japanese advance in small marine separators so that they would be unable to develop sufficient combat potential to risk an attack on Alfa Laval's large marine separators. This was particularly important since the profitability was in the large separators.

IBM

Since IBM claims to sell solutions and not products, it has chosen to segment its market by commercial type: banking, insurance, processing industry and transportation, so as to be able to tailor its solutions to more specific problem areas.

Each segment is then divided into sub-segments. Transportation, for example, could be divided into road, rail, air and sea.

Investing time and analysis resources in the right segmentation variables is a necessity. Some common bases for this are segmentation by:

- End user
- Product
- Geography
- Customer size
- Purchasing motivation

MARKET DEVELOPMENT

Once one has carefully considered one's market segmentation and selected the segments to be concentrated on, one must then follow developments in the different segments.

The market development for personal computers has been like this:

Personal computers delivered, Western Europe, 1984–86

Sector	Numbers 1984	Growth (%)	Numbers (1985)	Growth (%)	Numbers (1986)
Commercial	943,000	50	1,411,000	33	1,880,000
Scientific	139,000	23	171,000	23	210,000
Home/hobby	3,755,000	−18	3,096,000	−6	2,900,000
Education	320,000	43	458,000	−39	280,000
TOTAL	5,157,000	−0.5	5,136,000	2.5	5,270,000

SOURCE: International Data Corporation (IDC), May 1987.

35

As we can see, conditions are tough on the personal computer market, which demands great flexibility of market actors. Producing PCs on the basis of forecasts seems completely senseless. The only sound policy here is to manufacture on the basis of real demand all along the production chain—the just-in-time approach.

It also seems highly sensible not to be overdependent on a PC segment, but to have several irons in the fire.

TECHNOLOGICAL DEVELOPMENT*

These days, one can achieve a devastating competitive edge by using technology as a weapon. But you have to exploit the possibilities.

> *Everything should be as simple as possible, but no simpler.*
> (Albert Einstein)

Simplicity as a design principle is a secret of success in many areas. Nature itself is strikingly simple. The incredible multiplicity of living organisms arises, for example, from the simple DNA 'instruction code'.

DNA consists of only four elementary building blocks (nucleotides) combining in different ways to encode 21 simple amino acids. These amino acids then combine to form proteins. The enormous wealth of species comes from the enormously large number of amino acid sequences. There are no complex, specialized instructions. If there had been, living organisms would be highly specialized and unable to adapt to environmental conditions.

The first electronic computers were simple. From the 1950s till the 1980s, however, development took place only at the price of increased complexity, and the trend has been toward ever-more-complex instruction sets. So dominant has the technique of complex instruction sets been that practically all computers developed during the last twenty years have been so-called CISCs (Complex Instruction Set Computers).

At the end of the 1970s and the beginning of the 1980s, researchers began systematically producing a complete picture of how computer programs are executed. The result was astonishing. The research showed that the complex instructions were hardly used at all. The greater part of the time, the computer executed simple instructions such as loading, saving and goto's. Twenty percent of the instructions

---

*MAIN SOURCE: *HP Precision Architecture—A New Perspective.*

were executed in 80 percent of the time. This unexpected predominance of the simple instructions was in clear opposition to early assumptions about how computers should be designed. New avenues opened up for computer designers.

Hewlett-Packard

Encouraged by their discoveries, Hewlett-Packard researchers began the search for a computer technology in which their new understanding of how computers work could be used. Central to the new technology is a simplified and much smaller instruction set. Computers that use the new technology are termed RISC (Reduced Instruction Set Computers).

With a simple instruction set it becomes possible to build in instructions directly in the hardware, thus exploiting the higher speeds offered by new circuit technology.

While the competition (IBM, DEC and others—though IBM has an RISC computer, the IBM PC RT) continues to build new computers with the old technology, Hewlett-Packard are developing an entirely new generation around the simplified instruction set of the RISC model, coupled with the latest gains in hardware and software technology.

The result is *HP Precision Architecture* which has moved Hewlett-Packard up to a new S-curve.

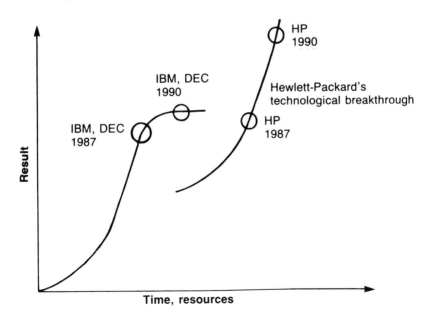

The *S-curve theory* states that at the beginning of a development project, a great deal of time and resources are invested for very little result. Then there is a technological breakthrough, followed by large results achieved with small investments of resources. After a time, results diminish in relation to further investments. The only way of recreating a positive development is to break the S-curve, but companies are often reluctant to do this since the beginning of a development phase is so slow.

Hewlett-Packard's Precision Architecture is based on a technique that stresses simplicity. This basic simplicity results in improvements in three areas:

- Shorter design and development time
- Lower manufacturing costs
- Greater reliability.

A simpler design is easier to produce. A simple instruction set eliminates the need for a microcode. Also, the system uses fewer components. The simpler design entails a shorter development time. Years spent at workstations can be shortened to months.

Since there are fewer system components, the manufacturing process becomes shorter and simpler: the simpler a computer is, the simpler and quicker it is to build. And when it is built, it is very reliable: fewer components means that there is less to go wrong.

THE SIGNIFICANCE OF THE PRODUCT LIFE-CYCLE FOR MARKET SUCCESS

Handling one's business philosophy, one's operations and one's products according to the basic principles of the product life-cycle is more important than ever before. The reason for this lies in the increasing speed of change.

Take an example. On Thursday, 30 July 1987 I read in a newspaper that Apple's turnover for 1987 was estimated at four billion US dollars. Of this, the company calculated that half would come from two personal computers, the Macintosh SE and the Macintosh II. These machines were released as late as in March 1987.

When asked in July, Apple Chairman John Scully said that the Macintosh II had been produced in six weeks. This was so that Apple could come on to the market before IBM launched its new PC series IBM PC/2. In all honesty, Apple cannot have started from scratch:

38

much must have been prepared—but it is an achievement nevertheless.

The product life-cycle consists of various phases, which place different demands on company market action:

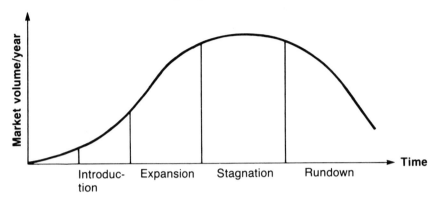

The preparation phase

Requirements in this phase may be:

- A developed feeling for what possibilities the market holds
- Information on the competition environment
- What products and services would beat the competition in the market.

This is the starting point of a company's development. It is then necessary to plan allowing great freedom of action and hopefully making sure at the same time that opponents' freedom is reduced. (Everything is relative, according to Einstein.)

If market introduction is planned carefully with the aim of avoiding or hampering the competition, things become easier later on. The plans that are made should exploit any existing possibilities for building up one's combat potential right from the start (see also Chapter 4, Analysis of ourselves).

The introduction phase

The introduction phase involves creating oneself a bridgehead for a powerful offensive later on. The main principle is that the introduction should be a rapid one, so that the function and quality of the product are experienced by the customer as 'right'.

If volume can be generated quickly and at a low introductory price, so lowering the total cost level per unit, then this should of course be

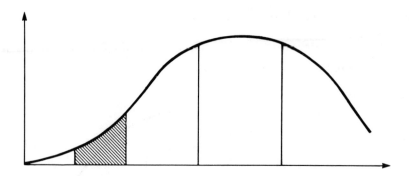

done. What is achieved by this is that the company's combat potential increases and competitors' eagerness to enter the same area diminishes because they read from the low price level that profitability is poor. One's own company has managed to create a low-cost position affording better and better competitiveness.

Where there are several products each needing to be introduced, choose the most unique: concentrate forces on that and let the others slipstream it. Concentration of forces is necessary because the profitability of a newly launched product normally looks like this:

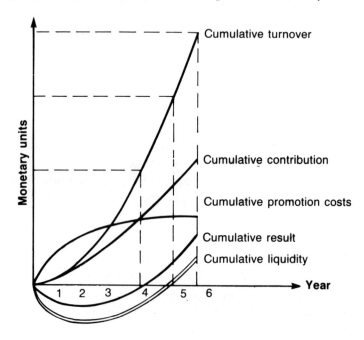

(SOURCE: Gunnar Dahlsten, former Executive Vice-President, Swedish Match).

The expansion phase

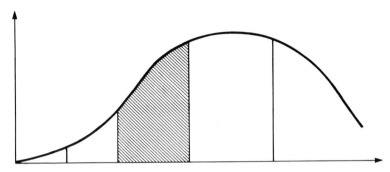

In the expansion phase, one concentrates forces on becoming market leader. Ample investment is necessary, so that there is sufficient capacity in all the sectors of the production and distribution apparatus the company has elected to engage in.

Now is also the right moment to round off one's market offer with supplementary products and services. The company's success will be so obvious in the expansion phase that even if competitors have not reacted before, they will do so now. Thus it is important, during the earlier phases, to have built up an intelligence organization that can indicate what the competition is up to (see also Chapter 5, Competitor analysis) so that one can in good time parry any steps taken against the company.

The expansion phase requires a high degree of flexibility and creativity if one is to keep the lead.

In the 'shake-out' phase towards the end of the expansion phase, companies or products that have not managed to generate enough combat potential have to leave the market, since growth falls off at the same time as competitors if the market invests frequently as if growth would continue to infinity. The shake-out phase thus more than confirms Darwin's theory of the survival of the fittest.

The stagnation phase

Correct action during the other phases of the product life-cycle means that one can now reap the harvest of one's efforts.

Economy of combat forces, cost-effectiveness, rationalization— this is the main rule for success in the stagnation phase.

Electrolux springs first to mind as a prime example of a company that is enormously successful at dealing with a stagnating market.

41

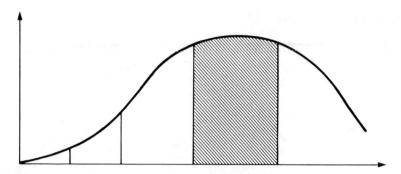

Within a short time of buying up a company, Electrolux has pared away all the fat and streamlined the operation with its own:

- Four factories become three
- Two purchase departments become one
- Fourteen different basic components become six, and so on.

However, the numbers of distribution channels and product variants the customer can choose from are retained. Rationalize internally, retain freedom of choice and flexibility in the market—an art that is both excellent and simple. (See also Chapter 4, Analysis of ourselves.)
Remember:

Everything should be as simple as possible, but no simpler.
(Albert Einstein)

The rundown phase

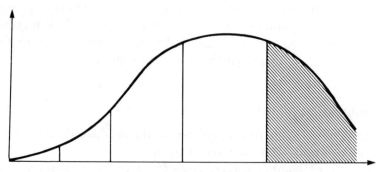

In the battles of old, cavalry was deployed against a retreating opponent. If you were able to retreat in an orderly manner, that is if you held together both physically and psychologically, you managed quite well against the cavalry. However, if the retreat was disorderly, flight turned into panic under the advancing cavalry and a bloody massacre was the result.

By planning the retreat carefully, thinking through *what* we must tell the troops and *how*, we fulfill the requirements of an orderly retreat.

In the computer industry it is increasingly common to manufacture machines in which the performance and number of functions can be increased by exchanging or adding a number of key components. The transition from the computer the customer bought to the next computer the customer will buy thus becomes a gentler one, and it is no catastrophe to buy the 'old' computer exactly when the 'new' one arrives. The computer company first sells a computer, then a number of boosters or performance raisers, and then a new computer, a number of boosters and so on.

This is an inspired way for the computer company to achieve efficiency and competitiveness throughout all phases of the product's life cycle, and is at the same time the material expression of the computer company's perfect planned retreat.

PORTFOLIO ANALYSIS

A business unit—the Strategic Business Unit (SBU)—is an operative unit that

- sells a defined group of products or services
- to an identifiable group of customers
- in competition with a well-defined group of competitors.

In most cases, the borderlines between different business units are not as crystal clear as one could wish. The products, for example, may be completely different but many of the customers and many of the competitors may be exactly the same.

When one has arrived at the important definitions of one's various business units, it is time to establish, for each unit, strategies that harmonize with the company as a whole. The goal is a well-balanced portfolio of different activities each with differing prerequisites.

Lecturing on strategy at the beginning of the 1980s, ASEA Executive Vice-President Percy Barnevik outlined how he intended to restructure the group:

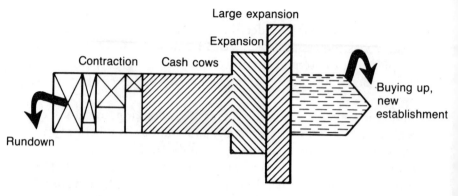

ASEA's goal was to transfer resources from units and products with a poor market outlook through rundown and contraction to units and products with good prospects through expansion and acquisition.

The company's cash cows are low-investment, high-profitability units or products which generate the capital necessary for financing the restructuring of the group.

Two widely used models for portfolio analysis are the Boston Consulting Group (BCG) model and the General Electric/McKinsey (GE) model.

The BCG model

The BCG model is very easy to understand and use. It is based on two premises:

- *The experience curve*, which states that unit cost decreases by 20–30 percent for each doubling of cumulative volume/experience. The greater the volume relative to competitors' the lower the costs, which gives better competitiveness
- *The product life-cycle*, which states that market competition is less heavy at the beginning of a product life-cycle and freedom of action considerably greater. We should therefore in the introduction phase work harder than our competitors to become the market leader.

The *cardinal rule* is to concentrate on growth markets. By putting more effort than competitors do into some company problem children, these will grow faster than competitors' products.

One will thus run down the experience curve faster than competitors do and, on account of one's size, will become a more attractive supplier and business partner.

When the market eventually stagnates and everybody's freedo[m]
action shrinks, one is well-placed to exploit one's position as m[arket]
leader.

Growth of the market

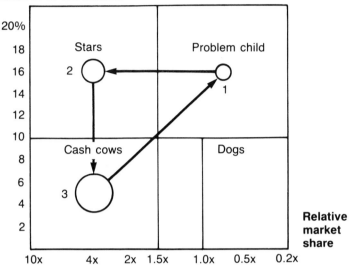

The model is really a cash flow grid. By working out how much
surplus liquidity the cash cows generate, one can plan how many new
products and/or activities the company can afford to invest
energetically in.

The next figure shows the result and the liquidity situation in the
various boxes in the BCG model:

Growth of the market

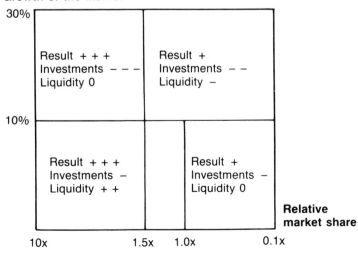

This figure tells us that the products or activities in the problem child box require more capital than the result is able to self-finance. This means that we get negative liquidity. In the star box, the result balances the investment and liquidity is thus neither positive nor negative. In the cash cow box we have a liquidity surplus since the result is now considerably larger than the need for investment. Lastly, in the dog box we have a small result surplus and small investments that cancel each other out in terms of liquidity.

The Electrolux use of the BCG model deviates from the main rule of concentrating on growth industries.

Electrolux buys up companies which, like itself, are operating in stagnating fields. However, when Electrolux buys up a number of dogs the result is a fine cash cow anyway. In this way Electrolux achieves greater volumes than its competitors. This, coupled with the fact that Electrolux is world rationalization champion, leads to greater and greater competitiveness.

I consider the BCG model in all its simplicity to be a good one to apply to various products or business units and to use with other strategy models as a basis for discussing and analyzing one's operations.

The GE model

The GE model employs two strategic variables: *market attractiveness* and *competitive position*:

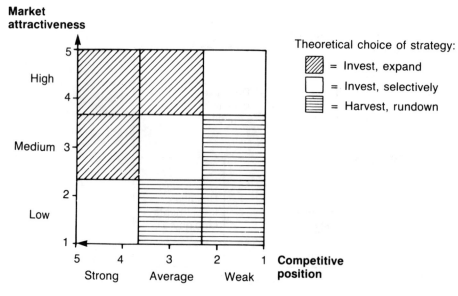

Some common factors determining whether a market is attractive for a company are:

- Market growth
- Market size
- Profitability
- Intensity of competition
- Seasonal variations

- Size of competition
- Frequency of new products
- Technological development
- Legislation
- Buyer concentration

The competitive position depends on the following factors, among others:

- Relative market share
- Absolute market share
- R&D capacity
- Marketing and distribution
- Quality, image

- Product/service range
- Position of product in life-cycle
- Technological level
- Capacity utilization
- Capital turnover

After deciding which factors regarding market attractiveness and competitive position apply, one can then weight these factors (total weight 1.0) and score from 1 to 5 (5 is best) how well the company's various Strategic Business Units do on each factor. The result might be as follows:

Market: Foodstuffs (part-segment)
Market Attractiveness

Success factors	Weighting	Points (segment 1)	Σ	Points (segment 2)	Σ
1 Market size	0.25	4	1.0	4	1.0
2 Profitability	0.2	4	0.8	3	0.6
3 Growth	0.2	5	1.0	2	0.4
4 Competition intensity	0.2	2	0.4	5	1.0
5 New product frequency	0.15	3	0.45	2	0.3
	Σ1.0		3.65		3.3

Market: Foodstuffs (part-segment)
Competitive ability

Success factors	Weighting	Points (segment 1)	Σ	Points (segment 2)	Σ
1 Product quality	0.2	4	0.8	5	1.0
2 Delivery service	0.2	5	1.0	3	0.6
3 Product range	0.1	3	0.3	4	0.4
4 Trademarks	0.1	3	0.3	3	0.3
5 Development capacity etc.	0.1	2	0.2	3	0.3
	Σ1.0		4.2		3.8

We then enter the position of the two Strategic Business Units in the GE model. The size of the circle shows the size of the market and the size of the pie slice shows our market share. The placing of the two SBUs in the GE grid is arrived at by drawing a line to the right from 3.65 on the market attractiveness axis and a line up from 4.2 on the competitive position axis. Where the lines cross is the center of the SBU. Repeat for the second SBU.

In this case, the *product portfolio* assumes the following appearance:

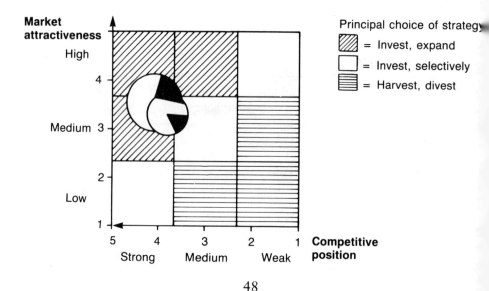

48

We now have a rough theoretical picture of the chief strategies to be applied to the different SBUs in our company using the GE model. Of course we have to discuss the SBUs thoroughly before deciding on any strategy, but this must not turn into an academic game.

If we wish to improve the position of our SBUs in the model, we now have clear indications of where it will pay to place our punches. The higher weighting a factor has, the greater the result of an improvement in score will be.

Personally I start by trying to see what the company looks like on the BCG model and then look at it from the perspective of the GE model. I use the result as a basis for discussion, not a basis for decisions.

Some reflections

Talking of success factors reminds me of a list that Bo Ekman (formerly responsible for VOLVO's strategic planning and now Director of the Swedish Institute of Public Opinion Research [SIFO]) showed during a lecture on strategy at the beginning of the 1980s:

Ten different ways of bankrupting a company
   (1) Errors in business idea
   (2) Errors in technology
   (3) Errors in the industry
   (4) Errors in marketing
   (5) Errors in the plant
   (6) Errors in efficiency
   (7) Errors in pricing
   (8) Errors in the organization structure
   (9) Errors in administration
  (10) Errors in financing

Not a bad checklist, and I hope others may also have use of it.

IMAGE AND POSITIONING

The image our company and its products presents may consist of solid facts, but much depends also on psychological influence. 'A theatrical comedy can have able actors who do a fantastic job on stage, and the performance can end with a ten-minute standing ovation. But the public don't come because the performance has been savaged by a few theatre critics who haven't been handled right, or who for various reasons enjoy criticizing.'

The company's image in the eyes of customers, competitors and society in general depends likewise on the degree of success in putting over the excellence of its various parts:

- Product image
- Service image
- The retailers' image
- Management's image
- The production image
- The company's image
- Attitude to society
- Employee relations.

We thus need to establish a psychological plan of operation. This is how the Testologen market research people say a corporate image should be created:

- Activity dimensions, type
  —on the advance
  —active promotion
  —extensive advertising
  —active product development
- Confidence dimensions, type
  —an industry leader
  —well established
  —competent staff
  —large company
- Economy dimensions, type
  —large resources
  —positive growth in results
  —competitive prices
- Product dimensions, type
  —technically excellent products
  —high quality.

Digital

I long wondered why Digital achieve such good press coverage. Reading a number of their press releases soon reveals the secret. In one of the many releases with which they flood the newspapers, it says (following an introduction saying what it is all about):

DIGITAL EMPHASIZES MANUFACTURING
INTEGRATION WITH INDUSTRIAL COMPUTER FAMILY

BOSTON, Ma.—March 24, 1987—Digital Equipment Corporation today announced a family of industrial products and services based on its VAX computer and networking architecture, as well as marketing agreements with leading factory automation vendors

---

The Corporation's President is then quoted on how fantastic Digital is:

'Integration is the key to maintaining a competitive edge in manufacturing,' said company president Kenneth H. Olsen, 'and it is based on excellence in networking. The industrial family greatly extends our ability to provide solutions for our manufacturing customers. This makes Digital the only computer supplier to offer a full range of systems, applications and services based on a single system and networking architecture.'

The release then describes in detail what is new, and then has another Digital employee speak about how fantastic the corporation is:

'The MSIS program is a vital component of our industrial offering,' says David Copeland, Group Manager, Manufacturing/CIM Marketing. 'Our software services group's ability to integrate applications within the Digital computing architecture provides a total manufacturing solution. It is this ability to create custom solutions and integrate them into a customer's organization that makes Digital unique among computer suppliers.'

The press release ends with the following lines:

Digital Equipment Corporation, headquartered in Maynard, Massachusetts, is the world's leading manufacturer of networked computer systems and associated peripheral equipment, and is the leader in systems integration with networks, communications, software and service products.

Getting good press coverage was clearly no more difficult than that. The secret was to write the article oneself, both facts and value-judgments, and hope that the journalists were not of the critically scrutinizing type.*

Hard Rock Cafe

When the HRC opened in April 1985, expectations had, through the mass media, been built up way above reality. The HRC could not live up to these unreasonable expectations, with the result that within a few months the papers became as negative as they had been positive. Much of the criticism was indeed justified, even though there were also some exaggerations. Even when the HRC, with enormous effort, had got its operation under control regarding quality, service and cleanliness, the negative picture conveyed by the press lived on in most people's minds. Yet the true picture now no longer matched the one the newspapers had painted.

The Tuesday rock band evenings were the HRC's strongest segment. They became the turning point: the HRC rapidly established itself as the best place in Stockholm for listening to live rock music. If we are the best, we should tell people, thought the members of the strategy group, so they coined this slogan:

Hard Rock Cafe
—Where real rockers play

'Real rockers' are the most important words in the new slogan, stating as it does why people should go to the HRC and not to a competitor. Positioning is all about distinguishing oneself from the others. It is essential to be the first to communicate one's positioning, and if possible to find a position that the chief competitor finds difficult to imitate.

When the HRC went in for tourists as a target group, the new idea was introduced with the Hard Rock map and the 'ambassadors.' The map contained recommendations for places tourists simply must not miss when visiting Stockholm. The Hard Rock Cafe was included, of course, but also other good restaurants. The ambassadors also talked about their work in a special tourist program on Radio Stockholm.

---

* Now perhaps I'm being a little mean. Digital has skillfully exploited IBM's market weaknesses to achieve great successes, which has also made it interesting to write about Digital.

Spendrup

Spendrup's superb slogan 'the private alternative' is perfect positioning. Neither the 'State alternative', Pripps, nor the 'cooperative alternative', Wårby Springs, can do anything about Spendrup's positioning. The other competing private breweries are way behind, and do not have the same feeling for image development as Spendrup has.

Spendrup's consistent *image promotion* of the excellent qualities of *malt beer* as opposed to beer brewed from corn, maize and rice—*fruit beer*—is by no means an exact science, but very largely the result of planned myth formation.

The agricultural company

For a company in the agricultural industry, the market positioning was like this:

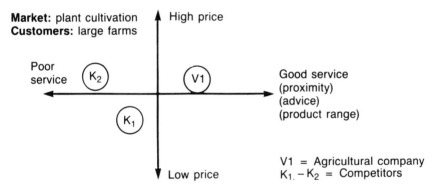

Market: plant cultivation
Customers: large farms

High price

Poor service K_2 $V1$ Good service (proximity) (advice) (product range)

K_1

Low price

V1 = Agricultural company
$K_1 - K_2$ = Competitors

The company was felt to be expensive, even though it gave considerably better service than its competitors. During a seminar that lasted several days, both the concrete problems and the psychology were thrashed out, and the following was the result:

- *The concrete part* An action plan which, using the company's superior competitive-edge organization, was to offer farmers improved cultivation economy.

   What the company could offer and its competitors could not was combined action from the different parts of its total organization.
- *The psychological part* It was necessary to convey to the farmers the message that the company stood for improved cultivation

economy. This was to be achieved through communications from our field representatives, through printed direct-mail information and through contacts with the media.

In the diagram used internally for getting everybody's agreement to the planned measures, price was therefore removed as a positioning variable and replaced by cultivation economy:

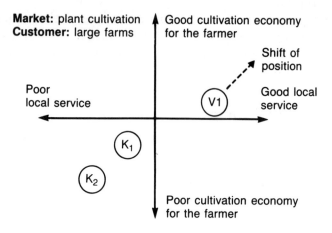

Volvo Cars

A now almost classical positioning diagram is the one Volvo Cars used for conveying to employees its vision of which way the company was moving:

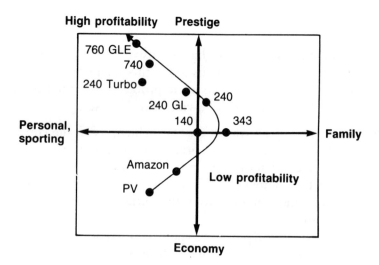

To survive as an automobile manufacturer, Volvo could not remain in the gray middle position. It was forced to differentiate itself from the volume auto manufacturers. The private automobiles division therefore elected to move north-west! They concentrated on making the Volvo a personal, sporting, prestige car.

In this way, they also chose competitors: Mercedes Benz, BMW, AUDI—which were by no means easy to take on but easier than the Japanese armada in the volume auto segment (in the gray middle position).

SABA

SABA's four chain stores B&W, Tempo, Åhléns and Åhléns City had great economic problems. One was that their positionings in the market and in relation to each other were all too indistinct.

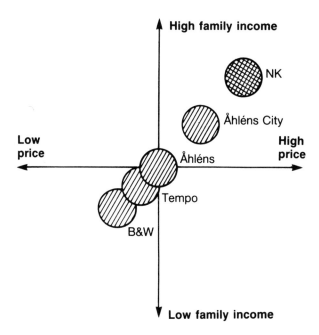

Renaming the Tempo stores Åhléns and simultaneously investing heavily in higher quality for Åhléns total offering laid the foundation for successful positioning of the chain stores.

There were now three chains with three distinct positionings: B&W became the low-price hypermarket, Åhléns the traditional store, but one quality level higher, and Åhléns City *the* store, which was to fight NK (Sweden's Bloomingdale) for that title.

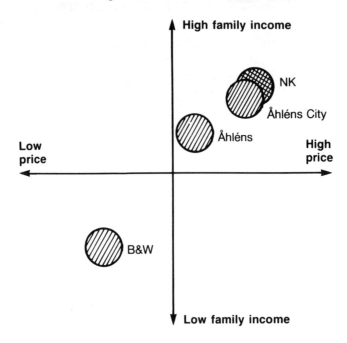

It may be difficult to limit oneself to two positioning variables. In such cases, a positioning model with four variables can be used.

The educational association

When a group deliberated on what variables to use for positioning educational association language training, it arrived at the following:

- Quality of course leader
- Quality of study material
- Quality of course administration
- Quality of group selection and competition.

Drawing the association's position as a reference point and then adding competitors' positions relative to this gave the following picture:

The association was in a very strong position compared to competitors, but it had so far been bad at communicating this, either internally or out to the market. In its planned marketing activities, the association therefore decided to promote its better market offer.

Market: Language training
Geographical area: Smallish urban area

V1 = Educational association
1 = Another educational association
2 = Smallish language consultant

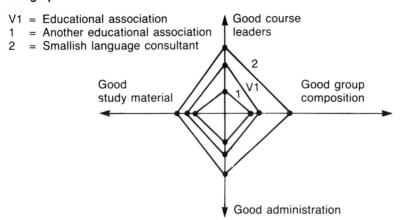

Market: Language training
Geographical area: Smallish urban area

V1 = Educational association
2 = Fairly small language consultant

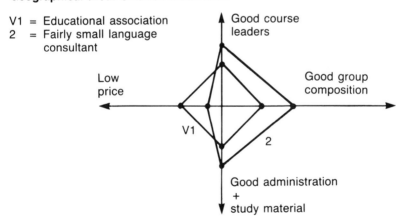

The association was inferior to the fairly small language consultant, but it was discovered that price as a positioning variable had been overlooked. By combining quality of administration and quality of study material, room was made for price in the positioning model and hence a fairer comparison was obtained.

The education association found that it was superior to the language consultant as regards price level but inferior in other respects. It was therefore decided that when processing the same customers as the language consultant, the association would concentrate on the price-sensitive customers while at the same time working hard to level out the differences in the quality of its market offer relative to the consultant's.

3 Customer analysis

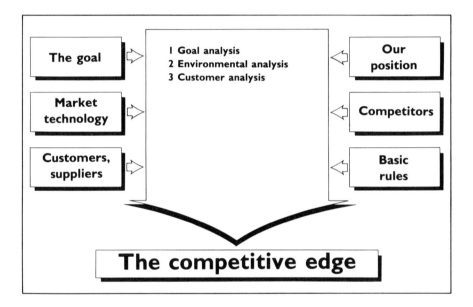

B.H. Liddell Hart, one of the great military talents, has in his studies of military battles throughout history, established that: 'of 280 battles, it is only in six cases that the victor has won through mainly direct methods. In all the other 274 cases, it is chiefly through indirect methods that decisive victory has been won.'

Indirect strategy is about seeking victory on the battlefield through deployment of one's strength against weak sectors or in secondary operational areas. Do not take the bull by the horns; bring him down by surprise attacks on his weak points.

According to indirect strategy, the opponent must be confused and must fail to understand what is happening until it is too late. One gets an opponent to disperse his forces and defend less important sectors while one prepares an attack against his weak points.

Indirect strategy can be summarized in four principles:

- Use of indirect methods to force the opponent to divide his forces
- Surprise through choice of unforeeseable actions
- Deployment of strength against weak sectors
- Decision in secondary operational areas, if this is possible.

There is no basic difference between beating a competitor and winning a battle, though of course one must be careful how one applies the indirect strategy. A number of semantic circumlocutions may be necessary before the choice of words in indirect strategy feels natural.

Let us look a little more closely at how superbly well IBM works *vis-à-vis* its customers: a textbook example of how to win a customer's confidence mainly through using indirect methods.

IBM

IBM says that it sells solutions, not products. To do this effectively, the corporation has divided its customers into fifteen main segments (branches), each with its sub-segment.

Over and above his basic sales training and general product training, the IBM salesman therefore receives branch-specific training enabling him, for example, to stand in as loans manager at the bank that is his customer. Appointment and training costs for an IBM salesman are reckoned to be about 150,000 US dollars a year. The salesman is then assisted by system specialists and product specialists who, in turn, often work on problem solutions for different branches.

Most important for IBM is to get a foot in the customer's door, to sell itself with the first installation. When this has been managed successfully, the massive IBM offensive rolls into action.

- Ask the customer contact what he thinks about his company's need for data processing
- Invite the customer contact and other members of the company to conferences and seminars that may be useful to them and, when the occasion arises, ask questions and make new contacts. This may concern anything from materials control seminars to conferences on 'Post-industrial Society' with, for example, Henry Kissinger as chief speaker and participants who include only members of the top management of large corporations. 'Everybody that counts was there'
- Invite the customer contact and others in his company to visit

with customers who have successful IBM installations—preferably to the most prestigious companies in the country

- Invite the customer contact and others in his company to come and look at IBM activities that may be of interest to him. These may, for example, include the project management system used when IBM launched its new-generation PCs over the whole world simultaneously, together with the experience the corporation gained from this launch
- Send articles, newsletters, house magazines, etc., that may be of interest to the customer
- The information gained by IBM in connection with these activities regarding the customer's problems and need of solutions is supplemented with information acquired by service engineers and systems specialists through working at the customer's plant
- Once a year IBM gathers together staff who work together with customers at an 'Account Planning Session' for a number of days. They go through the customer's general business situation, installed systems and how they have been working, who the customer's decision-makers are, etc. On the basis of this present-position analysis, an action plan is then drawn up covering the systems and products (solutions) the customer may need, who the competitors are, etc. The customer also takes part in these discussions, which is important when drawing up the plan. The customer has now been given a well-documented action plan for the next few years.

'What can happen,' says Buck Rodgers, 'is that the customer may come back a few years after an installation and be worked up because it doesn't meet performance requirements. IBM therefore documents the customer requirements and assumptions underlying a quotation, so that later discussion may be carried on in a businesslike manner.'

- Apart from this annual 'Account Planning Session,' IBM has 'Application Transfer Teams' that consist of specialists in the problems of different branches and the solutions IBM can offer.

  The team goes round to different customers and, together with the customer's staff, interviews managers from different function areas. This can take anything from two to eight weeks. The team maps how the customer is working presently and what changes may be necessary to make him more efficient. It is estimated that the team's ability to sell IBM solutions exceeds 75 percent.

'A wonderful partnership arises,' says Buck Rodgers. The wonderful partnership seems to be something from which many companies could learn much. As a customer, however, it is important to conserve one's negotiating strength so that one does not become entirely dependent on the supplier.

Let us study how to gain negotiating strength with regard to customers.* Our negotiating strength increases if the customer:

- Lacks a qualified alternative supplier
- Faces high costs if he changes supplier
- Lacks possibilities of backward integration
- Purchases a tailor-made product/service from us
- Earns large sums from the use of our product or service
- Enjoys high profitability and can pass on cost increases to his customers
- Has poor information on our competitive situation
- Has other aims than maximum pressure on prices
- Buys small quantities in relation to our sales turnover
- Is very dependent on the quality of our products for the functioning of his final product.

In any study of what customers buy, it is important to observe the different stages in sales planning:

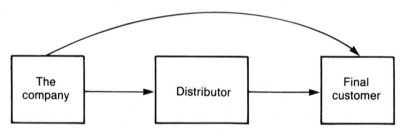

If one is selling automobile telephones, the customer analysis may show that:

The distributor buys	*The final customer buys*
• A good product	• Flexibility
• A good net margin	• Design
• Good marketing	• A security package
• Reliable deliveries	• Features
• Good service	• Ease of use

*SOURCE: Freely after *Competitive Strategy*, Michael Porter, Free Press. A division of Macmillan Publ. Co, New York.

Grasping the differences in customer requirements and offering the right solutions is the purpose of customer analysis.

(MAIN SOURCE: *The IBM Way*, Buck Rodgers, Harper and Row. OTHER SOURCES: *IBM—Colossus in Transition*, Robert Sobel, Times Books; IBM employees past and present; IBM distributors' reports on IBM)

4 Analysis of ourselves

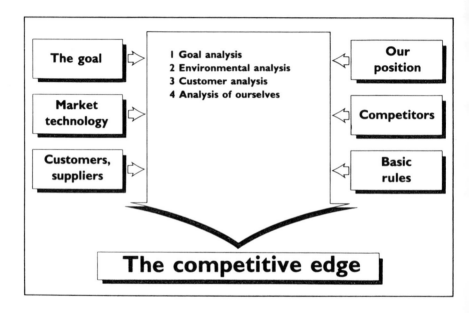

COMBAT POTENTIAL

The purpose in an analysis of ourselves is to generate a correct picture of one's own combat potential. In a military context combat potential is calculated using two of the factors that represent the general formula for strategy, namely the material factor (M) and the psychological factor (P) in the formula $S = u\,MPT$.

The obvious components of combat potential are:

- The armed forces
- Support
- Combat morale

- Leadership
- Organization.

However, these are not enough. Combat potential also includes factors to the rear of the actual battlefield and which can be exploited and committed to battle:

- Industrial capacity
- Demography
- Political system
- Economy
- Infrastructure, etc.

In commercial terms this means that when studying one's own strengths and weaknesses, one must widen the field of view. What forces can we engage outside the market we serve? Do we belong to a large, well-financed international organization with large research resources and advantages of scale regarding purchase, production and marketing?

On the other hand, do we have strong collaborators who can supply us with increased combat potential on our local market?

Combat potential is a combination of how well one manages to mobilize one's local resources with one's global resources.

Say that we manufacture electric trucks. To carry out the work tasks our product is intended for, we need access to computer power and suitable software for controlling the process. We can buy a standard computer sold by the thousands by a computer company, and buy standard software from a software company. We ourselves are responsible for the integration process which, hopefully, contains unique solutions. By doing it in this way, we exploit the knowledge and the advantages of scale that others have already acquired.

It is fashionable to dismiss the significance of scale advantages. Differentiation of one's market offering is advocated instead. My own view is that one should certainly differentiate one's market operation from those of competitors: this is partly what the fourth area of business philosophy, being unique and having the competitive edge, is all about. However, in a market with several tough competitors, one must also exploit all possibilities of achieving scale advantages.

Look again at the Spendrup example from the Introduction to this book. Spendrup went in for differentiating their offer and, through collaborators, gained experience and advantages of scale as well. A market exposed to heavy competition may look like this:

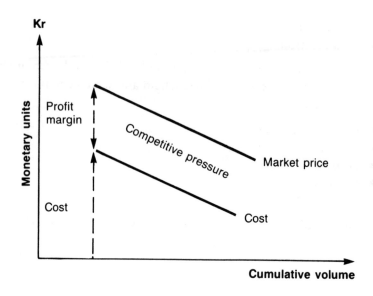

The rules of the game in a market or a market segment are often to invest in a *market share*. One should strive to become *market leader*, and this *quickly*, since the longer the delay, the more one is forced to invest.

POSITIONING

Positioning in the market relative to customers and competitors is an important element in developing the company's combat potential.

ACO's superb positioning in the 1970s of its skin care series is a typical flank attack. It consistently avoided its competitors' strengths and instead attacked 'holes' in the market. This is a comparison, from ACO's perspective, of ACO's marketing with traditional marketing:

(1) *Products:* often unnecessarily complicated, containing substances with no effect on the skin and with increased risk of allergy as a consequence.
   ACO's *philosophy:* simple, well-tried principles based upon medical knowledge.
(2) *Consumer market segmentation:* low awareness, low education.
   ACO: aware, high education.
(3) *Perfuming:* important/distinctive.
   ACO: less important/neutral/unperfumed.

(4) *Declaration of contents:* secret, 'to create a mystery'.
   ACO: openly declared or reported.
(5) *Packaging:* fancy design, gold, silver, sometimes poor technical quality'.
   ACO: simple design, high technical quality.
(6) *Publicity message:* emotionally oriented.
   ACO: product/technically oriented.
(7) *Media selection:* weeklies (company's message dependent on editorial environment.
   ACO: dailies, also evening papers.
(8) *Price:* high (high price can generate image of high quality).
   ACO: low price.
(9) *Emphasis in market mix:* personal sales to distribution channels and consumer (via cosmetologists).
   ACO: communication via mass media.
(10) *Distribution:* selective merchandise environments (beauty parlors, boutiques, department stores).
   ACO: selective technical environment (chiefly through pharmacies).

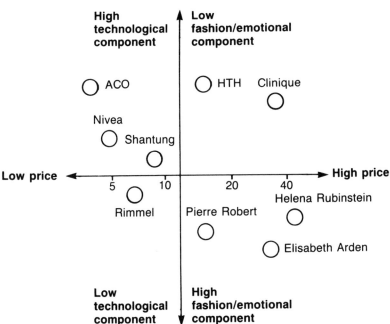

(SOURCE: *ACO Skin Care—A Case Study,* Göran Alsterlind, ACO International)

Following ACO's thorough preparation work, it was necessary to decide on how to communicate the company's uniqueness.

Should one assert one's advantages without comparison with competitors? Should one compare in general terms, or should a comparison point out competitors directly?

Many companies are too 'refined' to compare themselves with their competitors, or else they follow some antiquated rule stating that the market leader never compares himself with a competitor.

In the marketing war you have to be pragmatic and choose, for each case, the communication strategy that leads to long-term success.

COST-EFFECTIVENESS

When talking about rationalization, people usually quote the old saying 'work smarter—not harder.' Two examples of built-in cost-effectiveness follow.

The computer company

The traditional way of building computers is to buy a series. When the customer has outgrown the computer he bought, he buys the next size up, and so on.

To cope with the inconvenience entailed by the customer sitting there with an outgrown computer, special computer-leasing companies have appeared. Their ideal is to lease a computer (most often an IBM) to a large, forward-looking company. When after perhaps two years the company has outgrown its computer, the leaser can rent it to a smaller company, and so the game continues.

Another way of solving this growth problem is the Digital way. Digital links up the outgrown computer to a new one, and computer capacity can then be supplemented as required.

The most creative solution, however, is to design the computer right from the start so that performance can be increased or new functions added with minimal modification.

It is not hard to work out what this implies for the computer company in terms of savings in the development, purchasing, production and marketing functions, over and above increased security for the customer.

Traditional product development:

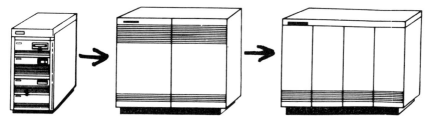

Creative product development:

Electrolux

When Electrolux buys up a competitor that also makes refrigerators, it coordinates the various operations as quickly as possible:

- Two research departments become one
- However, two design departments may remain two, since the different trademarks are retained
- Two assembly plants each handling two different basic designs are coordinated so that one plant handles one design and the other plant handles the other design
- Eight different sub-contracted refrigerator motors are reduced to four
- Five component factories become three coordinated ones. The other factories make components for other group companies.

Everything that can be rationalized is rationalized. However, with regard to the established trademarks of the different original companies, the multiplicity of product variants and local independence, care is taken not to disturb the market.

By thinking through the company's situation regarding *combat potential*, *positioning* and *cost-effectiveness*, we also get the answer to what strengths and weaknesses we presently have and what changes are necessary to reach the goal.

5 Competitor analysis

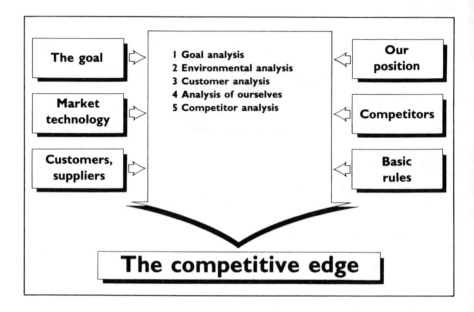

The loyal band shut the heavy oak door behind them so that the whole building thundered.

'The situation is serious,' said McCain.

'We know all too little about our competition. New ones are showing all the time, sometimes with darned good products comparable with ours—well, not quite of course, but very nearly. And the same old competitors are putting out one improved copy after another. Some of them aren't just copies, either: they're technological breakthroughs, like the Misshuubushi Black Eagle.'

'And they're not exactly sitting still, either,' said North. 'At ASGEA two of their salesmen just worked full-time for four months to land an order worth twenty thousand. In the end they installed it for a price way below our purchase price, and even so, the yen's gone up 30 percent in a year.'

'As retailers, we can't just sit on our butts any more and be served up lousy information from our supplier. Anyway, what does Data Inc. know about its competitors' retailers?' Cartland asked.

'Okay,' said McCain. 'It looks like we agree the situation is serious and we must do something fast. In two months we'll have a great chance to radically improve our knowledge of the competition. There's the Trade Fair—all the distributors will be exhibiting the products they carry.

'It's a chance we can't afford to miss, specially because it's a jubilee fair and they'll be blowing trumpets for their products. This means we can expect a big volume of product information, and we must grab it quickly.

'Do we agree, then, that our purpose in exhibiting, apart from selling products and making contacts as usual, will be to get information on our competitors?' McCain summarized.

'Not a day too soon,' commented Stallone. 'We just talk customer needs, customer needs, customer needs all the time, while the competition get in dig after dig at us.'

'Yes,' confirmed Rambo, 'It's time to put on the knuckledusters and—give it to them!' And he banged his fists on the table so it shook.

The temperature in the room rose rapidly and so did the noise, as one wild suggestion followed another. McCain, who had said nothing for a time, finally called the meeting to order and in the ensuing silence nearly whispered, 'Enough. Let's hear what Johnson has to say.'

'Well, gentlemen, let's do what we used to do in the forces,' said Johnson, an ex-intelligence officer. 'We need to be quite clear *who* our enemies are. Are they our distributors' competitors on the world market, or are they the distributors at home here? Then we must decide *what* we want to know about the enemy. And not just product information: we want to know how many salesmen they have—how many of these are experienced and how many are green—how well trained they are—what their sales ploys are, and their attitudes when they process customers—that kind of thing.

'The next step is to draw up a plan for *how* we find out what we want to know. How much can we learn when we're in uniform and when do we need help from our collaborators to find out?'

'What d'you mean—we're going in for espionage?' McCain asked.

'No, of course not. That's illegal,' Johnson replied. 'If you go onto the stand of our biggest competitor—and that's the Computer Group distributors—and ask the questions you want answers to, what do you think happens?'

'Question is, whether they'd let me onto the stand at all,' said McCain.

'Right,' Johnson answered. 'That is the question. But what do you reckon happens if you have a brother—and he really needs new equipment for his factory—if he goes in and asks legitimate questions?'

'I see what you mean,' murmured McCain. 'Go on.'

'Then we have to analyze the information we collected. Draw conclusions, see the right people get just the information they need. Next we have to form our hypotheses about the enemy. . . .'

Eastwood groaned, started waving his arms violently. 'Can't take all this military crap. Draw us a picture or something, use words an honest civilian can understand.'

'Okay,' said Johnson. He went up to the board and started to draw.

1 Who are our main competitors?
2 Objective: Basic information, strengths – weaknesses

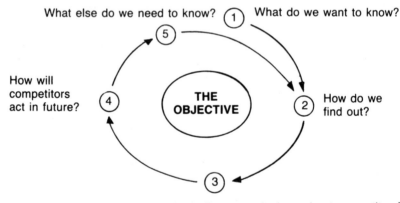

'Understand now?' asked Johnson, fixing his ice-grey eyes on Eastwood.

'Sure. Looks easy,' Eastwood answered. 'Why didn't you say so from the beginning?'

'Then, when we know the competitors' strengths and weaknesses, we smash them. We take over their best accounts, we break sales

72

records month after month and in a year's time we're sitting in Hawaii planning the next move against them!' said star company seller Caspberger.

'Anybody any objections?' McCain asked.

'No!' was the resounding answer.

The discussion went on for some hours, and the result was two tables: one showing both suppliers and retailers. The distributors had been chosen as the enemy, with the most important at the top of the list.

(Suppliers)	Distributors = 'enemy'	What do we want to know?		
		Turnover	Employees	Salesmen
1. X1, X2, X3	Ret. 1			
2. Y1, Y2	Ret. 2			
3. Z	Ret. 3			

Most of what was on this list could be filled in even before the Fair, from competitors' annual reports, by talking to salesmen, from the information material competitors' mail to customers, and so on.

A call to the Credit Information Center brought annual reports for the last three years, plus additional tabulated information including the following on the biggest competitor:

Trading Year	Turnover	No. of employees	Turnover/ employee
85/04–86/03	108,772,000	74	1,470,000
84/04–85/03	116,155,000	66	1,760,000
83/04–84/03	105,454,000	56	1,883,000
82/04–83/03	71,282,000	53	1,345,000

It was also found out who owned the competitor, which is very important when assessing his combat potential. Since the owner was listed on the Stock Exchange, the group was asked to mail the last three years' annual reports.

The reports presented the group business idea and philosophy, and there was a good description of member company operations. Now the different pieces had been collected, it was possible to start piecing them together.

The list was then expanded with 'dossiers' for each competitor, to which more information was successively added. One complete list looked like this:

COMPANY NAME:	Computer Group Inc.
COMPANY FORM:	Wholly owned subsidiary of large group. Agent. No own manufacture.
ADDRESS:	Smith, Jones Inc., 1234 Main Street
BOARD MEMBERS:	Eugene W. Smith, Zorro Agnosticon, Betty Pilaster
TRADING YEAR:	5.1–4.30

	86–7	85–6	84–5
TURNOVER (million dollars):	120	160	140
PROFIT (million dollars):	15	24	18
NO. OF EMPLOYEES:	73	70	62
TURNOVER/EMPLOYEE (million dollars):	1.64	2.29	2.26

BUSINESS IDEA:	Sale of process computers, software and peripheral equipment for manufacturing companies with strict demands on high reliability.
SALES OFFICES:	New York, New Orleans.
STANDING:	Large stable company, well-established, long tradition. Very strong position of product A8.
SALES TACTICS:	Tend to promise more than they can deliver, specially with product A1. Very active sellers, follow up every deal carefully, focus on own sales

arguments. Good price/performance.
Talk 'dirt' about competitors.

MARKET ACTIVITY: Use large adverts for direct
confrontation with our product
Area 1.
Often run campaigns following
Proctor Publicity's standard format.

PRICE POLICY: Great flexibility—large discounts
possible. List prices somewhat above
ours.
Prices of US products follow dollar
rate. Prices of Japanese products sink
with the yen rate, but follow poorly
upwards, the latter because Japanese
put higher priority on market share
than on profitability.
(List-price list and discount rates
attached.)

SALES FORCE: Significant resignations noted. A
small number of salesmen have long
experience. Generally limited product
knowledge. Product-specialized
salesmen. Often give 'know-all'
impression.
Salesmen have been dissatisfied with
salary policy, but this now put right
after internal convulsions.

SUPPORT
ORGANIZATION: Very high class support. Slightly
overdimensioned due to sales slump.

REPRESENT: AKEZO, HIITACHA (JAPAN)
MOTOROLA (USA)

COMMENTS: Mass drop-out of salesmen during
last trading year has been made good
through new appointments. Combat
morale good and improving. Much
stress on advertising and other sales
aids, to compensate for sales force's
lack of experience and to increase

combat morale. Tendency toward poor price/performance because concentrating more and more on their Japanese suppliers, who are disadvantaged by exchange rate development. Are thoroughly on the offensive, but less competitive now than a year ago.

The second table was like this:

Supplier	Our product areas			
	Area 1	2	3	4
1. X1	A1, A3, A8	—	—	—
2. X2	T4, T8	P4, P3	P8, P11	—
3. X3	—	—	—	K1, K4

The table shows which supplier's products the company was fighting in different product segments. This overall picture was filled out with 'files' for each product area, where it was clear what suppliers/products the company was competing with.

A week before the Fair all the salesmen and a few hand-picked staff were called to a general meeting. McCain described the situation and began to show the summaries which were being filled in.

'But much is still to be done,' he said, and showed his list of some remaining questions. 'Not everybody can do everything, so I propose that we together go through who is best suited to find the answer to each question.'

The intelligence plan produced for the Fair and adjusted at the meeting is shown at the top of the opposite page.

As to the more sensitive areas of information collection, these were planned by McCain and Johnson. During the Fair, Johnson led a team that received the information from everybody involved. After a rapid analysis, the intelligence plan was adjusted to cover new problem areas that had arisen.

After the Fair, printed information was compiled, and this included

Intelligence need (questions)	Method	Source	Responsible
1. Product introductions from Distributors 1, 2, 3 etc.	Reconnaissance/ questions/literature study	Ret.'s stand	AB. CD. EF. GH. IJ. KL.
2. Changes: supplier/ distributor	Reconnaissance/ questions/literature study	Ret.'s stand	MN. OP. QR. ST. UV. WX.
3. Distribution channels – Invoicing – Development	Reconnaissance/ questions/literature study	Ret.'s stand	
4. Representatives' sales talk, attitudes	Reconnaissance		

observations made by salesmen and others. Conclusions were drawn about how the market was developing and about competitors' strong and weak areas. Action plans were made for avoiding the competitors' strong areas and striking against weak points. Care was taken that everybody involved received feedback from the operation according to their needs.

What I have just described is based on a genuine intelligence mission. For deeper understanding of how to work, I shall now go further into the process. I shall try to describe reality, without getting into ethics. Although many readers will certainly question the ethics of part of what is described, I stress that I have been restrained when I write about reality.

A central part of the market war is of course to collect information about competitors. Quantities of information can be got quite legally from Annual Reports, for example. Other information can only be obtained using alternative methods. Examples of this are realistically described in the book *Spycatcher* by Peter Wright, Viking Publishers.

Often information pours over one, and one has only to listen and put two and two together. An excellent place for this is an aircraft, where colleagues not infrequently discuss their company's doings. If one pricks up one's ears, one can hear much of interest from the seat in front.

THE 'SHOP TALK TECHNIQUE'

The following example is based on the 'shop talk technique'. It can be used at trade fairs, meetings with old acquaintances, etc. The example has no connection with reality and the names are fictitious. It gives a realistic picture of what may happen next time you run into a former colleague who knows how to ask the right questions.

The train started with a jerk, waking me from my reverie. On the other side the Inter-City had just come in. I leaned back in my seat as the train glided out of the station. It had been a hard day. Our new Executive Vice-President had vented his spleen over everybody at the meeting: if results didn't improve during the next quarter, he was going to fire the whole of the management.

He had risen slowly, leant over the massive oak table, pushed back his tall chair and hissed at me: 'That goes for you too, Mister Erik Asp.'

For me too, who had worked night and day to get our cars sold! Our cars with their engines like old threshing machines, thirsty and impotent.

The door of the compartment slid open with a bang and there stood a pale individual with engineer's horn-rimmed glasses. The look behind the thick lenses sought the empty seat opposite mine.

'This seat free?' he asked.

'Sure, go ahead,' I said, recognizing Palle, Palle Wester from SAAB.

'Erik, great to see you! Must be four, five years,' Palle answered. He deposited his large black briefcase and stretched out a hand.

'Fancy you turning up like this—how are things?' I said.

'Oh, so-so, how about you?'

'Just fine, I'm off to Jönköping. Where're you bound?'

'Same here,' said Palle and hung up his well-used brown cord jacket on a hook.

'Great. These train trips knock the hell out of me as a rule but it'll be fun to chat a little,' I said and lit a Marlboro.

Inhaling deeply I leant back and asked: 'Well, you still live in Jönköping, too, then—weren't you on the way to the lab in Trollhätten?'

'No, I had a chance, but my wife couldn't—you know, her job and everything.'

'Your wife—Eva, isn't it—how is she?' I said.

'Eva left me a year ago. Said I had to choose between her and my job. I was tired of all the squabbling so she took her things and went to live with her mother.'

'You must have a terrific job if that was your choice,' I said.

'Research on new engines, materials and things. Yes, well, you must

78

know a lot about that kind of thing,' said Palle and ducked as the train entered a tunnel.

'No, I was never in that line. Anyway, I left SAAB three years ago. I'm doing other things now.'

'Left SAAB!' Palle leant forward in surprise. 'Just when we're doing so well. D'you know, we made 320 million profit last year, and 50 percent of that was from the US market alone.'

'Well I'll be—so Lövgren's done that well?'

'No-o, that clunk isn't with us any more. We've a whole new team. Sophia Fixitall is Head of Marketing now—she's really done wonders.'

'You don't say. And what wonders are you doing?'

'My oh my! We've been working full pressure. See, Friday, we cracked a really tough nut. Champagne party all evening—even the President looked in and congratulated me.'

'But that's great. You must be sitting pretty after a success like that.' I saw that Palle could hardly stop himself from talking about his proud discovery.

'Yes, well it's a secret as a matter of fact but if you keep it to yourself I can tell you. We've found out how to make the explosion absolutely homogenous with nothing left over. One hundred percent clean exhaust and half the fuel consumption. How's about that!'

I was dumb with astonishment. It was every designer's dream and Palle's gang had made it come true! Invented the perfect auto engine. . . . Must play dumb and inquisitive.

'We-ell, congratulations!. . . You giving them away for Christmas?'

'No, no, still at the prototype stage. We have to solve the cooling problem. Neither ordinary steel nor aluminum can take 1800–1900 degrees.'

'No?—Why does it get so hot?' I asked with the most innocent look imaginable.

Palle was burning with enthusiasm now he had the chance to tell somebody what his researcher's brain was teeming with.

'Well, for one thing combustion is much more intense and for another we have to get the engine up to 10,000–11,000 revs for it to work best.'

'How come? Don't know much about it, but doesn't an engine work best at low revs?'

'Yeah, well we inject the fuel through an electron field so we load every particle with a negative charge. Then you put a field potential into the combustion chamber between the plug and the piston and hey presto everything lines up in neat rows just as you want and combustion is total.'

'. . . Now I have to strike while Palle is hot . . . ,' I thought, and went on in my best dumb-cluck style.

'Yes, but don't you get shocks if you have current flying about in there?'

'Oh no. Okay, we run at 600,000 volts, but only a couple of microamps, so there's no risk at all.'

'Not bad—but what do you use as fuel?'

'Ordinary gasoline, but it works just as well with diesel oil or kerosene. We reckon we can use any fuel there is.'

'Aren't there any problems with the fuel?'

'Sure, the whole engine seizes if there's the slightest trace of sodium silicate in the fuel.'

'This seems fantastic. When can you start production?'

'Well, we got to apply for patents, test a lot of things and set up a new production line in the Linköping factory, but we hope it'll be ready in about twenty months.'

The train thundered on at the same pace as my brain. . . . Cancel our decision to buy shares in Bosch, their injection will be dead in two years. . . . Put in patent applications in every country we can think of for injection techniques using electron fields. . . . Hire Sophia Fixitall as head of Marketing. . . .

We also have to work out a crisis plan in case they get there first. . . . Can our Shell contact fix a dash of sodium silicate in the petrol? High r.p.m. demands expensive ball-bearings, we should step up our collaboration with SKF. . . . Half of SAAB's profit comes from the USA. They're sure to make their big push there and leave Europe open to us. . . . Re-budget and go in for different markets, provided the dollar stays quiet. . . . Get somebody taken on at their Linköping factory. . . . It'll be interesting there the next couple of years.

Poor Palle, he must be worried as hell about what he's been saying. . . . Best to taper off the interest now.

'Well, Palle, not that I understand much of all this, but it's good to hear things are going well for you. Had a vacation this year?'

'Only a week, but oh, boy! I was out sailing in the skerries. Sun every day and perfect sailing conditions.'

'You don't say. Didn't know you were a sailor. Now you'll have to give me some tips on what boat to buy.'

'A. . . .'

And Palle was on to his favorite topic. Soon he'd have forgotten he ever mentioned his discovery. He never found out I was working for Volvo. A year later the SAAB management would discover to their surprise that their invention was already patented, Volvo would have grabbed Europe from under their noses and would have hired their star Sophia.

SUN TZU AND COMPETITOR ANALYSIS

There is nothing new in obtaining information about competitors which, after analysis, is used to make the right moves in the struggle for the market.

Five hundred years before Christ, the Chinese general Sun Tzu wrote how to win wars—*The Art of War*. A chapter of the book is devoted to how to build an intelligence organization with five different types of agent. The importance of access to information on terrain, on the enemy and on one's strengths and weaknesses permeates the whole book.

Sun Tzu says in the book: 'Know your enemy and yourself; in a hundred battles you will never be in peril. When you are ignorant of the enemy but know yourself, your chances of winning or losing are equal. If ignorant both of your enemy and of yourself, you are certain in every battle to be in peril.'

The reason the wise general wins the battle, says Sun Tzu, is that he beforehand has had the good sense to obtain reliable information on the enemy's situation. He gets this information through persons who know the enemy's situation well.

For this purpose there exist five types of agent that can be appointed, says Sun Tzu. These are natives, insiders, double agents, expendable agents and permanent agents:

- *Natives* are persons recruited by us from among the local population
- *Insiders* are officials who have been dismissed from their work, or who have made mistakes and been punished. They are persons who have not advanced to higher posts, or persons who see that they can take advantage of troubled times. Ask them what they want for their information and bind them to us
- *Double agents* are enemy agents whom we appoint. If we pay them very well, we can use them against the enemy

- *Expendable agents* are those to whom we deliberately give incorrect information. When the enemy seizes them, they give information which they believe to be correct. For this reason, the enemy believes the information and acts accordingly. When the enemy then discovers that the information was false, he executes the agents
- *Permanent agents* are those who continue to give information. We select persons who are intelligent, gifted and have the ability to establish contact with persons near to the ruler.

Thus do we obtain continual knowledge of the enemy's moves and plans.

'Generally in the case of armies you wish to strike, cities you wish to attack and people you wish to assassinate, you must know the names of the garrison commander, the staff officers, the ushers, gatekeepers and the bodyguards. You must instruct your agents to inquire into these matters in minute detail.

'If you wish to conduct offensive war you must know the men employed by the enemy. Are they wise or stupid, clever or clumsy? Having assessed their qualities you prepare appropriate measures.'

Thus Sun Tzu in 500 BC. What is important, and Sun Tzu stresses this, is that we have to get to know the competitor's key people, their strengths and weaknesses and their importance and influence in the company. One should not, of course, assassinate the competitor's key men as was done in Sun Tzu's time.

Readers of documentary spy thrillers remark that in the methods used by the intelligence services of various states very little has changed since 500 BC.

Sun Tzu's book is a best-seller in Japan and the main contents are quite in line with Japanese operations on the world market. Sun Tzu speaks of the direct method *cheng* and the indirect method *chi*. He defines cheng as what fixes and distracts the enemy and chi as flank attack, surrounding attack and what decides the battle.

A chi operation is always unexpected, unusual and unorthodox, while a cheng operation is more open.

In war, politics, business, as in love, it is important to have a good balance between cheng and chi. The basic principle is that chi action should dominate.

What has all this got to do with competitor analysis? Successful chi action requires much more information about the opponent than cheng action does, since in chi one is often playing a psychological game with the opponent. One seeks the spot at which he lays himself open, and concentrates one's forces there. One makes every effort to surprise him, which presupposes that one has good knowledge of him.

KEEP ONE STEP AHEAD

I shall now discuss mainly the principles for an intelligence service, stressing competitor analysis; but the principles hold good for all information processing regardless of whether it concerns markets, customers, suppliers, technology or competitors.

Intelligence must be run with an eye to the future, since our knowledge of competitors is to be used for improving our future market operation.

How the new knowledge of our competitor is to be used is not fixed in advance. The result of analysis can lead to:

- Buying the competitor
- Cooperating fully or in part with the competitor
- Asking to be bought by the competitor
- Going on the offensive against his weak points
- Changing one's market mix to avoid direct confrontation with the competitor.

Creativity and general ingenuity should govern the steps that are taken. What often happens in the market is the following:

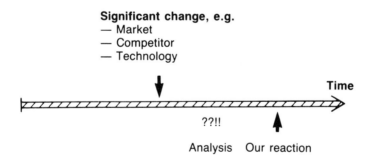

The figure above shows an organization caught with its pants down and now forced to produce suitable measures under heavy pressure of time. Instead, they should have goal-oriented their information gathering, which after analysis and the formulation of hypotheses would have led to their taking steps before their opponent did, so that he would have been the one to be left behind.

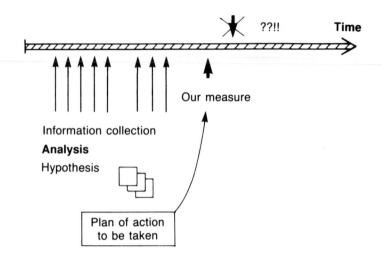

It follows from the figure that one first acquires and analyses information. Next one forms hypotheses and then acquires more information. Only then does one implement planned steps.

Who our competitors are is not always self-evident. In the case of the Hard Rock Cafe, it was decided to go ahead quickly with the strategy plan for who the main competitors were. It is not certain that they really were the main competitors, but the ones chosen served as electric hares for effectivizing the operations.

The ideal, however, is to make a careful analysis of the competitive forces within the market. In most markets, turbulence accelerates, which means that our friend of yesterday can be our enemy today. In our marketing, product development, internal organization and routines, it is important not, if we can help it, to make it easy for anyone who may conceivably start competing with us.

A concrete example of what I mean is the case of the motivation courses which Claus Möller started running for SAS, but SAS then started similar courses themselves. We can moralize and say that SAS 'pinched' the courses from Claus Möller, but I think this is a wrong appraisal. If Möller's course idea is right and SAS can and wants to run motivation courses, why should SAS not do just this? Why should a transport company not organize motivation courses internally and externally if this fits in with its overall business idea? If a company selling knowledge has a business idea without built-in 'barbed wire obstacles' of various kinds such as part-ownership, patent, unique competence, unique network, then one has to take the risk of others starting to do similar things.

84

As the starting point for a discussion of who one's competitors are right now, who can be expected to be so tomorrow and what can be done to prevent increased competition, Michael Porter's diagram below works extremely well:

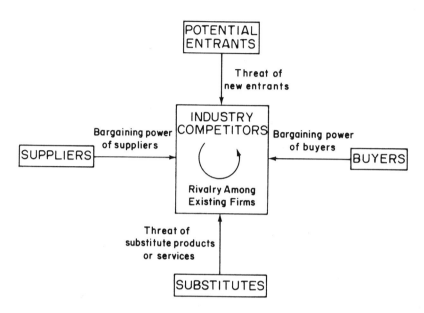

(SOURCE: Michael Porter, *Competitive Strategy*, Free Press. A division of Macmillan Publ. Co, New York.)

I have already mentioned that the collection of information must be goal-oriented. The information we need is more than the purely financial. Hard facts about competitors, e.g. turnover and number of employees, production capacity, etc., must be filled out with 'softer' variables such as those that appeared in connection with IBM's fundamental values. McKinsey uses the so-called 7S model, illustrated on page 86, when carrying out organizational changes for clients.

Since all successful competition is largely a psychological game, the model gives a good indication of what to look for in the opponent. Study the competitor's strategy, then, and his organizational competence. How are the various company units deployed in relation to each other? What system, i.e. routines and processes, controls the operations of his organization? How able are his staff? What is the leadership style and what the shared values?

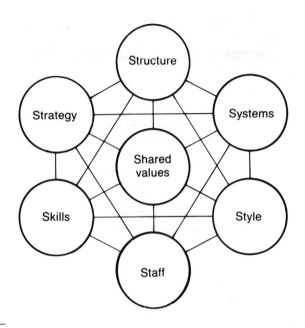

(SOURCE: The 7S model: Peters and Waterman, *In Search of Excellence*, Harper & Row Inc.)

WORK ROUTINE FOR THE INTELLIGENCE SERVICE

Work routine for the intelligence service:

The goal

Intelligence is a continuous process. It is important that the goal of the operation governs this process all the time. When defining the goal, bear in mind that the purpose of the information acquired is *ultimately* to evaluate the opponent's options so that one can then select one's own correct option. Underlying future work, therefore, is one or more fairly well-established hypotheses regarding the opponent's options.

Direction and collection

Direction means that we decide what we are looking for and ask pertinent questions that will give us relevant information. We then have to decide what methods and sources we shall use for collection, and who of our people will be responsible for obtaining the intelligence.

Processing

Perhaps the hardest part of intelligence is assessing the information collected and producing the correct appraisal. If we think carefully through the preceding steps, the work of processing the information can be significantly reduced.

Imparting

It is essential to give the right people exactly the information they need, quickly and comprehensively, if the purpose is to be achieved. We shall later go through the various steps in more detail, and shall examine how to formulate hypotheses in Chapter 7 (Main competitors' options).

DIRECTION

As a basis for choosing the type of intelligence needed, one believes 'something' about the opponent's future action.

This is what I mean by forming one or more hypotheses. A hypothesis is based on a number of known puzzle pieces plus assumptions regarding what pieces are missing. We try to work out what the complete puzzle really looks like.

Direction means that we decide what we are looking for, our *intelligence requirements*. We do this to check that our hypothesis regarding the competitor's future action is correct and to obtain the detailed information needed for us to make the correct moves against him.

Our own intelligence requirement regarding the competitor may appear like this:

(1) Product information on products X, Y, Z.
(2) Invoice volume and development for each distribution channel.

(3) Pricelists, discounts.

(4) Combat morale among salesmen and service engineers.

(5) Staffing and planning of service organization.

(6) Competitor's collaborators within the product area.

These requirements are for basic information. Intelligence needs should also cover how the opponent may act in the future, i.e. they should be linked to the hypotheses.

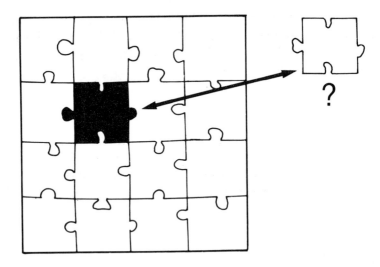

COLLECTION

Collection has three aspects:

- Methods
- Sources
- Internal responsibility.

Methods

- *Reconnaissance* Study your opponents' behavior in the field. What, for example, do their sales points look like? How do their staff behave? Describe the competitor's total market offering at the sales point. Attend the same fairs and exhibitions, the conferences the competitor organizes for his retailers and customers—anywhere competitors show, you go too.

- *Questioning* Question everybody who knows anything about the competitor: our employees (e.g. salespeople, product managers, service engineers), customers, suppliers, retailers, collaborators, other competitors and the competitor's staff (both present and ex-).
- *Literature study* Study annual reports, product information sheets or catalogs, articles in the daily and trade press, TV and radio interviews, multiclient studies, inquiry reports, consultants' reports, doctoral and predoctoral theses, credit information, staff and customer magazines, quotations and tenders, pricelists, patent applications, etc.

   To simplify getting hold of written information, search national or international databases, or buy the services of an 'information broker.' Use press-cutting bureaux for newspaper coverage.
- *Hire your competitor's key executives* This is an efficient way of finding out what one wants to know. The closer one gets to where today's and tomorrow's decisions are made—and to where there is decision material—the better. If the person you get hold of is also highly operative, then you are well up on your competitor.

   This may be considered unethical, if the main purpose is to obtain information about the competitor, so ensure that you keep your own key staff, through a far-sighted staff policy. Remember also that the competitor may not have your moral sense.
- *Cooperation* Cooperation with other companies and organizations (including competitors) implies both giving and receiving information. As long as you know what you want, you can get hold of very valuable information. Take care, though, that the partner's main reason for cooperation is not to gain information about your own company's operations.
- *Material examination* Examine competitors' products and service offerings. Map the quality and function of the products examined (VE = Value Engineering) and try to estimate manufacturing costs as well as distribution costs (VA = Value Analysis).

Sources

While processing the intelligence, one must also determine how reliable the various sources are. If at an early stage one thinks through what sources it is intended to use, and how reliable they are, the processing stage can be greatly simplified.

A rule often used is that, for a piece of intelligence to be considered as correct, it must be confirmed from two mutually independent and highly reliable sources.

Three groups of sources are:

- The competitor himself
- One's own organization
- Other sources.

The competitor himself

- Annual reports for some years back, plus the president's comments on these
- Product information sheets and catalogs
- Product advertisements, company advertisements
- Customer magazine
- Staff magazine
- Situations advertisements
- Articles in technical and economic journals
- Conferences, seminars, fairs and exhibitions
- Interviews in the media.

Our own organization

- The salespeople
- Product managers and service engineers
- The board
- Staff formerly employed by the competitor
- Information gathered at hiring interviews
- Other staff who know something about the competitor.

Other sources

- Customers (both distributors and final customers)
- Suppliers (of products, services and product servicing)
- Competitors' competitors
- Cooperation partners
- Various authorities
- Multiclient studies, trade/industry studies

- Market surveys, consultants' reports, public inquiries
- Daily newspapers, trade press, TV, radio.

The intelligence plan may, for example, look like this:

Intelligence need	Method	Source	Responsible, internally
1 Product info: product X,Y,Z	Reconnaissance/ literature study	Trade fair, competitor's stand	TA, BT
	Ask	Retailer X	KT
2 Invoicing and development for each distribution channel	Ask	Former employee salesmen: KT, AC	TA
3 Pricelists, discounts	Ask	Customer X,Y	KT, AC
	Literature study	Retailer Y	KT
		Former employee	TA
4 Combat morale (salesmen and servicing engineers)	Reconnaissance	Trade fair	TA, BT
	Ask	Salesmen: KT,AC	TA
	Literature study	Competitor's customer and staff magazines	TA
	Ask	Hiring interview	LK, TA
	Ask	Former employee	TA
5 Service organization, staffing and setup	Ask	Former employee	TA
	Ask	Customer Z	KT
	Literature study	Competitor's customer and staff magazines	TA
6 What co-operative partners have competitors for production area T?	Literature study	Competitor's customer and staff magazines	TA
	Ask	Retailer Z	AC
	Ask	Competitor X	AC
	Ask	Salesmen KT,AC	
		Chief responsibility:	TA

The plan described consists of parts of three authentic plans. What I am trying to put across is the feeling that one should use a number of sources for meeting the same information need.

It is, of course, easiest to ask one distributor or customer several questions about the competitor, but spreading the questions over a number of informants avoids making them feel they are being pumped.

In addition, the more natural the context where the questions are asked, the better. The questioner should have a genuine reason for asking, otherwise he risks suspicious counter-questions: 'Why are you asking?' Such situations can be somewhat hard to get out of with honor.

PROCESSING

Processing consists of evaluation and analysis:

- Evaluation of the reliability of the source
- Evaluation of whether the information seems correct (the facts are right)
- Evaluation of whether the information (intelligence) is confirmed
- Analysis of information used for assessing competitors' strengths and weaknesses (this chapter)
- Analysis later used for assessing competitors' options (see Chapter 7, Main competitors' options). Analysis is used here for constructing new hypotheses and comparing these with earlier ones about the competitor.

For assessing the reliability of the source, the following military grading can be used as a pattern:

(A) Entirely reliable
(B) Usually reliable
(C) 50 percent reliable
(D) Usually unreliable
(E) Reliability cannot be assessed.

And the factual correctness of the source can be graded as:

(1) Confirmed
(2) Probably correct
(3) Possibly correct

(4) Probably incorrect
(5) Incorrect
(6) Cannot be assessed.

One rule used is that where there are two mutually independent and highly reliable sources, the intelligence is confirmed. We assess the value of the information as follows:

We have four sources: a   b   c   d

of varying reliability   B   C   C   F

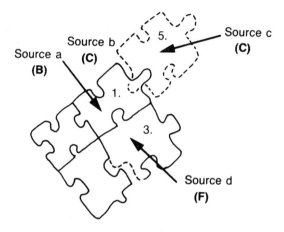

The figure shows that intelligence from sources a and b agrees completely, and the sources have good reliability. We thus assess the factual correctness as 1: confirmed.

The intelligence from source c does not agree with that from sources a and b, which is confirmed. The reliability of source c is C, i.e. 50 percent. We therefore assess its factual correctness as 5: incorrect.

The intelligence from source d does not fully agree with source a's and source b's as regards common details, but the reliability of source d is graded F: reliability cannot be assessed. We assess the factual correctness of the intelligence as 3: possibly correct.

For anyone who is upset by the military grading nomenclature, there is nothing to stop them from making their own grading scale.

One company has produced:

Source reliability:
(A) Sure
(B) Often sure
(C) Unsure.

Factual correctness of intelligence:
  (1) Definitely correct
  (2) Probably correct
  (3) May be correct (rumour)
  (4) Incorrect.

In one case, analysis of the intelligence gave the following picture regarding the competition:

  (1) The competitor's products X, Y, Z are equivalent to ours regarding the most important assessment criteria (detailed comparisons made).

  (2)

Distribution channels	Invoicing (mil. $)	Growth (%)	Market growth (%)
Retailers	5	0	30
Direct sales	40	20	20
Mail order	5	100	50

The competitors' progress with the retailers is poor due to the retailers' dissatisfaction with the service organization. This will become worse (see point 4). The competitor is successful with mail order sales as a result of great marketing efforts, but profitability is poor.
  (3) His prices are 10–15 percent below ours across the board. Discount rates resemble ours except for direct sales of over $500,000, for which he allows 25 percent discount as against our 15–20 percent. Detailed comparisons made.
  (4) Combat morale among the salesmen is very high because of new products X, Y and Z. Few remaining experienced salesmen; many new recruits during the past six months.
     Combat morale is poor among service engineers due to poor leadership and incorrect salary policy. Mass drop-out two months ago, of Service Manager's two closest men, plus three others, who all joined our competitor XL. The service organization is falling apart.

IMPARTING

Compiled assessments of competitors' positions, resources and options (consisting of freedom of action, tendencies, strengths and weaknesses) should be presented regularly. Some items, however, may be of such importance that they should be given to people concerned within the company in unprocessed form. Similarly, certain intelligence may, because of the time factor or high secrecy value, need special handling.

This is what the work routine for imparting information looks like:

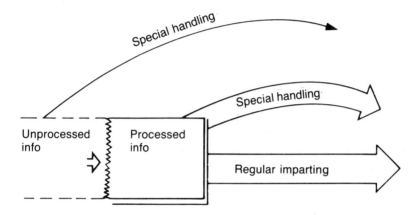

It is important for the imparting of information to be handled with discrimination. This applies above all to the assessment made concerning main competitors' options (see Chapter 7).

Some examples of how this imparting of intelligence works in practice are as follows:

- *Monthly Newssheet* describing competitor's development, new products, changes in his organization, campaigns he is running, plus some general conclusions from this. The Newssheet should be kept brief, mailed to many people, and should indicate that there is access to considerably more detailed information about the competitor.

  The Newssheet can include an interest coupon where the recipient marks his need for further information. This is a way of successively teaching the organization to keep a better and better look-out for what the competitor is doing and saying, and of training the organization to draw conclusions from various events

- *To the sales organization* the intelligence function gives continual summaries describing how the competitor works in the field, his different product offerings, his general or his product-specific strengths and weaknesses and, most important, 'How to sell against the competitor's different product offerings.' Attending the various sales meetings, you can give and obtain information, and pinpoint the need for more
- *To top management* information is given on the competitor's financial development, organizational changes, changes of strategy and cooperation, research results, investments and how he is viewed by the market. This is done regularly at top management meetings, board meetings and so on.

When something very important has occurred, unprocessed or processed information is given immediately to the persons concerned.

Organizations possess whole oceans of information that one should gather and impart, raw or processed, to whoever needs it most. If a company's intelligence service is to function, then one must make sure that people have good use of the information given them. They will then also be prepared to impart information themselves. This is the simple basis of an intelligence function that functions.

THE COMPETITOR'S STRENGTHS AND WEAKNESSES

Let me conclude this chapter by showing what an analysis of IBM's general strengths and weaknesses could look like:

IBM

Strengths

Organization
- Has many times greater financial and staff resources than any competitor
- Worldwide sales and service network
- Market leader by virtue of its large market shares, capital base, economies of scale, cooperation, and marketing and management resources

- A winner's attitude throughout the organization. Buck Rodgers seems almost surprised if a customer chooses something other than IBM. What went wrong? Didn't the salesman find out what the customer wanted? Weren't IBM's arguments any good? Was the price wrong? Etc. That competitors could quite simply have better hardware and solutions is something that seems not even to occur to Buck Rodgers.

  IBM is quite simply the best: that's all there is to it.

Market dominance
- IBM is well established at company and computer management levels
- Is good at drawing attention away from competitors and to itself. (When IBM speaks, everybody listens)
- If IBM goes in for an operating system or a network, this usually becomes a standard for the industry. Competitors have to toe the line
- Is good at getting dealers to agree to IBM's conditions: 'This is how IBM views cooperation.'

Products
- Many different product solutions for different problem areas
- Good at 'fixing' weaknesses in its product range.

Weaknesses

IBM's weaknesses are many, but I will confine myself here to raising what is by far the most important reason why Digital, Hewlett-Packard and other computer companies have been able to take market shares from IBM in the minicomputer section during the past few years.

A comparison between, for example, IBM and Hewlett-Packard for 1988 shows that IBM has five product families that compete with a single Hewlett-Packard family.

Hewlett-Packard vs. IBM positioning

If a customer buys a computer from the IBM S/36 family and the company's information processing volume increases by 40 percent a

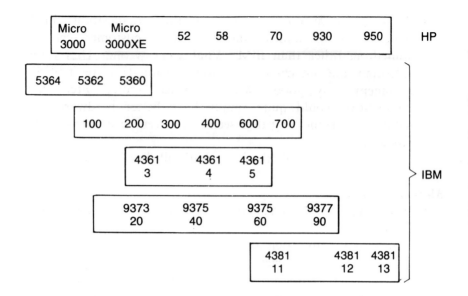

year, which is common, then after a few years he has to change to the next computer family—IBM S/38. After a few more years, he has grown out of the S/38 family and has to change to the 9370 family. Since the customer cannot, unfortunately, just move his computer programs between families, great amounts of time, resources and planning are necessary if everything is to work properly.

Within the Hewlett-Packard 3000 family, on the other hand, programs can be moved freely between the various computers and, in most cases, a smaller model can be updated to a larger one with more features and performance, with only fairly small modifications to the computers.

This is, of course, impossible if you are moving from an IBM S/36 to an S/38 and then to the 9370 family.

As IBM dominates the computer market to such an extent, competitors are forced to ensure that their computers can communicate with IBM equipment. However, IBM has never needed to put any effort into making its own computers communicate with competitors'. IBM's attitude to its competitors has been the same as that of the legendary Gothenberger who, asked what Gothenbergers say about people from Stockholm, replied, 'Nothing, if we can help it.'

For this reason, many of IBM's competitors are better at communicating between different computers. There is thus some justification for the joke that if you want to make two IBM computers communicate with each other, you buy one from an IBM competitor and put it between them.

Though I have described some of IBM's very serious weaknesses, we must remember that the corporation is fully aware of them and is working hard to put them right. It would not be surprising if, in a few years, IBM had succeeded. If any of IBM's competitors had these weaknesses, they would really be in trouble—which says a lot about the extent of IBM's enormous strength.

6 Comparison of forces

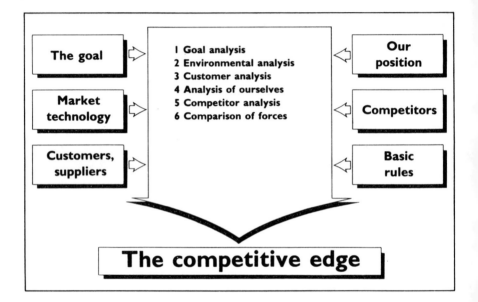

When making a comparison of forces or strengths between one's own company and one or more competitors, it is important to observe as far as possible the total operative effect regarding a given point of time and a given combat terrain. The total operative effect can be calculated by weighing together the four Ps of the market mix:

- Product (e.g. quality, features, packaging, service, brand names, guarantees, range)
- Place (e.g. distribution channels and coverage, warehouse locations)
- Price (e.g. list price, discount credit terms)
- Promotion (e.g. advertising, personal sales, sales promotion, publicity).

100

Important are also the efficiency of our organization, our market positioning and how well we have succeeded with our external maneuvering.

A good job in the earlier five phases of the BATTLE model means that we now know what market segments we need to make strength comparisons for. We know what success factors apply in each segment. We know who the main competitors are and we have a good knowledge of our own and the competitors' strengths and weaknesses.

However, before moving on to the strength comparisons it is important to know exactly what the point of them is! The purpose of strength comparisons is to map one's own and competitors' freedom of action and thus to obtain a good basis for discussing the competitors' options, plus what alternatives there are for achieving market success.

A strategic comparison of strength at company or product level goes like this:

(1) Start by deciding on the market and competitor that are to be the subjects of the comparison
(2) Then note down market success factors
(3) Order and weight the market success factors
(4) Now draw in one's own position relative to the competitor for each success factor.

The current position picture now obtained of one's own and the competitor's strength positions at company level may look like this:

Company X position vs. Company Y

Market success factors

	Weaker		Equivalent		Stronger	
	1	2	3	4	5	6	7
Products				○			
System				○			
Organization						○	
Prices					○		
Costs					○		
R&D							○
Delivery time	○						

One then makes strength comparisons for other competitors of interest.

When in this way one has gained a good grasp of one's overall strength position, it is time to make comparisons at product level, on the lines already described. Such a comparison may look like this:

Product X position vs. Product Y

Market success factors

The comparisons of strength we have now made at company and product levels are static comparisons.

If the time factor is taken into account and we weight the various competitors' most probable steps and our own planned steps, the expected position at company and product levels can be described as follows:

Company X position vs. Company Y

Market success factors

102

Product X position vs. Product Y

Market success factors

	Weaker		Equivalent		Stronger	
	1	2	3	4	5	6	7

Sensitivity
Flexibility
Time factors
Reliability
Prices
References
Documentation

———— Present position – – – Future position

The above strength comparisons are from one area of business in one of Sweden's largest companies, where I helped make comparisons against all their biggest international competitors and for all key products—a total of more than 100 comparisons produced by the entire marketing staff.

At a large international sales conference we went through the majority of the comparisons, with a lively discussion as a result. The strength comparisons were then kept by the salesmen so that they could check how well they agreed as regards each local market, and so that any local corrections could be made.

These local comparisons gave the marketing staff valuable information which, after processing, was forwarded to other company functions for further analysis and action.

Hard Rock Cafe

Work on the strategy plan went on under pressure of time. This led to the comparison of strength becoming more important than normal, since the subsequent steps of the BATTLE model were also concentrated here. In the case of the HRC this meant that, while analyzing the results of the strength comparison regarding these points, the consultant tried to work out what action the competition might take in the near future. The consultant also ensured that the measures decided on were suitable for both present and future market and competition situations.

For the Rock Evening segment, the comparison showed that the company had built up a strong position. It was therefore decided to take the steps that would secure the present competitive superiority. The weak points were the HRC's general image and what was called the 'social infection image', that is, what-my-surroundings-think-of-me-if-I-say-I've-been-to-the-HRC.

The image problem had been noted earlier when pondering what external maneuver was necessary. So, once more, there was a discussion of what measures were required if the HRC in general and the Rock Band Evening in particular were to give the image the company thought it deserved.

Market: 'In' restaurant
Market segment: Rock evening
Competitor: X

Success factors	Weaker		Equivalent		Stronger		
	1	2	3	4	5	6	7
Bands						○	
Atmosphere					○		
Acoustics							○
Image of place				○			
Social infection image				○			
Food						○	

For another key segment, 'Weds, Fris and Sats 10.00 p.m.–2.00 a.m.', the success factors were different and the segment was also more problematical, most of the team being of the opinion that its position was a big minus.

Dividing 'position' into two parts brightened the picture:

- The *impulse position* was defined as a place people go past and spontaneously take in when they are out in town
- The *position* was defined more geographically as how easy it was to get there and how many people lived in the immediate neighborhood.

If a person had decided to go to the HRC, it was easy to get there. We therefore needed to make the HRC so attractive that people had decided on it before they left home.

The greatest problem apart from the ever-present image question was social contact and what I somewhat disrespectfully call picking-up.

The most important step for improving the HRC's competitive

Market: 'In' restaurant
Market segment: Wednesdays, Fridays and Saturdays 10.00pm – 02.00am
Competitor: X

Success factors	Weaker		Equivalent		Stronger	
	1	2	3	4	5	6	7
Impulse position							
Position							
Image							
Concept							
Social contact							
Picking-up							
Environment							
Staff							
Staff idea							

position on these points was to arrange a dance license. However, many other changes were needed too, to give the restaurant more life and movement, since the HRC is supposed to be a place where things happen all the time.

By defining the problem and giving the direction, a basis had also been laid for a program of action to move the HRC out of an inferior position and give it the competitive edge.

The type of staff considered best suited for work at the HRC had been decided and now it was important during the new recruiting to explain clearly what the HRC stood for and what was expected of each new helper. At the beginning of September 1986 six people were recruited to leading positions: restaurant manager, kitchen manager, two financial assistants and two management trainees. These people continued, together with management, to implement the steps decided upon.

For existing employees it was important to keep explaining what the HRC stood for and what was expected of them in connection with the innovations.

Using the comparisons of strength, the HRC's competitive position had now been summarized. Because of time pressure, assessments were included of competitors' options and the restaurant's own alternatives when discussing the comparisons. The plan of action produced included all the steps of the BATTLE model, even though the later steps were treated somewhat summarily.

To go through the BATTLE model properly, however, when

comparing strengths, one should confine oneself to looking for one's own relative strengths and weaknesses.

What, then, was the final result for the Stockholm HRC? Bear in mind that a restaurant consists of an infinite number of small details that are pieced together to make a whole. Restaurant staff are individuals with ideas of their own. In this case, therefore, each change of detail had to be explained and justified in personal discussions with practically every single member of the staff. This meant that the process of change was rather a slow one. Communication out to the market, however, proved to be very effective, which meant that the public knew things were going well for the HRC before we ourselves really realized it!

Management continued to work toward the goals. After only a year, monthly sales had doubled and the result was positive. After nearly two years' very hard work, Anders Johansson left his post as Executive Vice-President in August 1987. A few other people in leading positions also left during the Fall. The new management partly changed strategy and, for example, stopped the regular live music. Sales and results continued well during the fall of 1987.

There are various approaches to communicating one's relative competitive superiority to the outside world. One can make indirect comparisons or direct comparisons with competitors, and here I would point again to the need to free oneself from burdensome rules. In the marketing war it is no good fighting with one's hands tied: one must be pragmatic and adapt to the market situation.

If the direct approach is chosen, then comparisons can be made with regard to a number of factors. These are not necessarily the ones that are most important for the customer: we can sometimes select the factors where we know we are superior to the competition. On facing page is shown how RESO, the Swedish travel agent, compares itself with the competition.

Personally I prefer the approach where one concentrates on comparing one or two factors between oneself and one's competitor. The comparison is then better focused, which makes communicating our message to the market easier. (See Vingresor's ad on facing page.)

Vingresor's price comparisons with selected competitors are palpable pinpricks, which are not so easy to counter.

The naive newspaper reader sees Vingresor's ad and remarks that Vingresor is cheaper than Fritidsresor. The more devious reader says that he knows what really lies behind this. Naturally, he says, Vingresor has been planning this for months. It made sure of booking

If it's a hotel card you want, what else need you know?

	Inter S Hotels Gold Bonus	Sara Hotels Business Card	Reso Hotels Stamgästkort
11th night free	★		★
Express check-in, check-out		★	★
Upgrade of room		★	★
Two for the price of one		★	★
Half telephone charges		★	★
Guaranteed reservation			★
Car rental rebate			★
Free morning paper delivered to room			★
Special offers in restaurant			★
Price per year	0:–	300:–	0:–

YOU'LL PROBABLY WANT TO KNOW HOW TO APPLY FOR THE CARD. THERE ARE TWO WAYS — EITHER PICK UP AN APPLICATION FORM AT ONE OF OUR THIRTY HOTELS, OR SEND IN THIS COUPON TO: RESO HOTELS, STAMGÄSTKORT, S-113 92 STOCKHOLM, SWEDEN.

NAME

COMPANY

ADDRESS

COUNTRY

RESO HOTELS

It's this easy for 2 adults and 1 child to save 1.285—this summer

Fritidsresor 8.620:-.

Hotell Mincete, Dubrovnik. Totalpris ...

Vingresor 7.335:-.

Hotell Mincete, Dubrovnik. Pris en vecka i dubbelrum med Vingresor från Arlanda lördag 18/7. Flygbolag Scanair.

its tours into a few hotels it knew the competition had also booked. Then Vingresor prepared colorful catalogs, but waited with the computerized pricelist until the competitor's catalog came out.

The company then lowered its prices for the selected hotels, and the agency that had the adverts ready and waiting simply inserted the fresh price comparisons.

Who was right in this case I cannot say, but I do know that in the marketing war you cannot be trusting: you have to make sure you plan for the nastiest tricks the competition can play on you, and also for the most improbable.

To continue with the example: in your contract with the hotel owner, ensure that you do not have your competitor in the same hotel. If this has to happen, at least set your prices so that you make it tougher for the competitor to make price comparisons to your disadvantage. And why not keep one hotel with rock-bottom prices up your sleeve? Who knows, you might need it sooner than you think.

Know your enemy and yourself; in a hundred battles you will never be in peril.

When you are ignorant of the enemy but know yourself, your chances of winning or losing are equal.

If ignorant both of your enemy and yourself, you are certain in every battle to be in peril. (Sun Tzu, 500 BC)

---

7 Main competitors' options

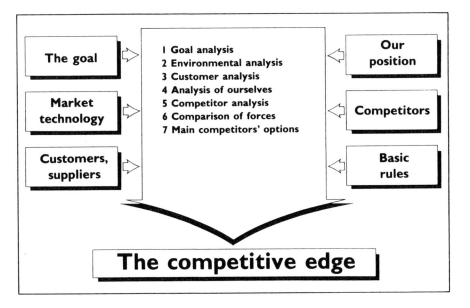

The goal	⇒	1 Goal analysis 2 Environmental analysis 3 Customer analysis 4 Analysis of ourselves 5 Competitor analysis 6 Comparison of forces 7 Main competitors' options	⇐	Our position
Market technology	⇒		⇐	Competitors
Customers, suppliers	⇒		⇐	Basic rules

The competitive edge

Late Friday evening, the telephone rings at the Spokane home.

'Sorry to call you so late, but I just have to talk to you,' says Wayne, who is Executive Vice-President of the METAL Corporation.

'What's your problem?'

'Look, together with the CRONOMANT Corporation, we have the whole USA market. We have 70 percent and they have 30 percent. Around ten months ago we found out they're investing in new production capacity. They're increasing capacity by over 60 percent at one go, and they're doing it in a market that's nearly stagnating. They're starting up in two months.'

'Yes, sounds as if you're in for a rough time. I just don't see why you didn't call me earlier. Looks like there's not another minute to lose. Can you get your Board together for a strategy meeting in your War Room, Monday or Tuesday?'

'If anybody doesn't come, he's a deserter—be shot at dawn,' said Wayne.

'That's the way. Get together all the information you can: market developments, technology, your and CRONOMANT's customers, your own strengths and weaknesses, CRONOMANT's strengths and weaknesses, so we have it all to hand at the meeting. And can you see to it that we get food and drink served in the room. We'll start 07.00 Monday morning. Another thing—do you have anyone in the company outside the Board who holds useful information about CRONOMANT?'

'Sure—we must get Nicklaus along. What he doesn't know about CRONOMANT isn't worth knowing. Same golf club as Ballantine, their sales chief. They play together a lot. When Ballantine wins, he's more uppity than usual. Entertains Nicklaus with how they're going to smash us to bits soon as they can start using their new capacity.'

'Sounds like we're going to have a couple of very interesting days. I'll stay at the Grant Hotel Sunday night. Pick me up 6.30 Monday morning, we can talk some more on the way,' said Spokane and put the phone down.

At the Monday morning meeting it was decided to go through the various steps of the BATTLE model, starting from the beginning with Goal Analysis.

The result of the Analysis went up on large flip-block sheets that soon started to fill the room. The analysis looked like this:

1. Goal analysis

METAL's aim is to retain its present share (70 percent) of a market that has an annual growth rate of only 3 percent, and to do so while maintaining high profitability.

'The aim looks unrealistic,' said Spokane. 'It implies that the greater part of CRONOMANT's increase in capacity would be unused, or would be sold outside the USA. CRONOMANT's aim must be to place the main part of the increase within the USA as profitably as possible.'

The others nodded their agreement. Brando gave a cunning look. 'Unless we help them export.'

110

The members of the meeting grinned at each other like wolves in a pack that knows it has got its prey surrounded. Spokane saw that they had begun to realize what they were really doing, and said in satisfied tones, 'Okay. Let's go on, shall we?'

2. Environmental analysis

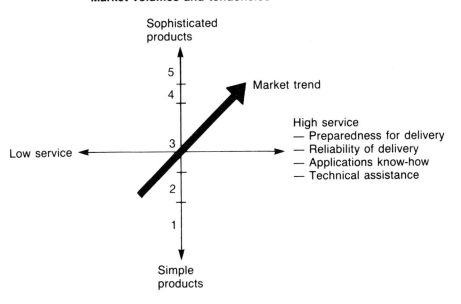

Market volumes and tendencies

Product area	Market size (%)	Growth (%)	Profitability
5	15	10	Very good
4	10	8	Good
3	35	2	Good
2	15	Negative	Poor
1	25	Negative	Poor

'Market development favors us—we're considerably stronger than CRONOMANT in areas 4 and 5, both of which are showing good growth and good profitability,' said Castelo.

'Yes,' said Ewing. 'And our competitive position is none the worse

111

for the fact that it's only in exceptional cases that CRONOMANT can offer acceptable quality levels in these areas. In practice, we're really alone.'

Position analysis gave the following picture:

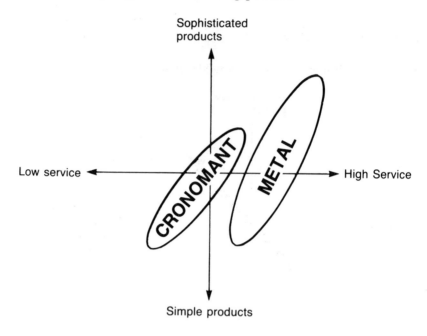

Wayne went up and pointed at the position analysis.

'Many years of conscious work have put us in a position where we should now be able to reap the fruits of market developments. The trend is getting clearer and clearer. While we've been working for this, CRONOMANT are still in nearly the same position as they were three years ago.'

Spoke asked, 'How about demand, for the different regions?'

Ewing produced the following picture:

'With our two factories in Los Angeles and New Orleans, we've got 50 percent of the market within easy reach,' said Ewing.

'And the picture's no worse for the Southern region—even more the Western region—being growth areas, which helps us. And there's a clear shift to the more sophisticated products there,' Brando added.

'The CRONOMANT factory's in Philadelphia, Northeastern region, so CRONOMANT has the advantage of the lower freight costs that show up in the simpler products in demand there,' said Wayne.

Market region	Market size (%)	Market growth (%)	Development by product area
Central	25	Negative	Overdemand for simpler products
Southern	20	3	Normal market
Northeastern	25	0	Overdemand for simpler products
Western	30	8	Overdemand for sophisticated products

'It's not by accident,' Ewing commented, 'that our customers located where we have our factories are buying products that are more and more sophisticated, and that they have positive growth for those of their products that have ours as important raw materials. We have a significantly stronger hold on them, which is making them see us as a partner in cooperation to increase their competitive strength, not just as any old supplier.'

'I think many of CRONOMANT's customers are a little jealous of ours. They'd like VIP treatment too, but *unfortunately* it's price that clinches the deal in the end,' said Castelo.

Spokane thought it was time to move on in the BATTLE model, so he wound up by saying: 'It seems that, together with CRONOMANT, you've achieved the perfect market division—from your angle. But what gets me is why in hell they're upping their production capacity by 60 percent. Seems mindless. Don't they read their market reports?'

3. Customer analysis

The conclusions from the customer analysis were as follows.

Many customers are under pressure concerning profitability because of the heavy competition between them. They can hardly take any appreciable rises in prices, but would in fact welcome, even encourage, a price war.

The number of customers is relatively limited. In total there are fewer than 100 in the USA, which means that we can visit them all personally in a short period.

Even though customers like to talk about 'the price' as the supreme buying factor, they are becoming increasingly dependent on first-class service, help with applications development, high quality, and dependable and frequent deliveries if they are to manage.

Whether the customer is buying simple products or more sophisticated ones, he needs a supplier who is as interested as he is in 'just-in-time' deliveries, top quality and finding new applications.

METAL's potential for offering customers the partner relationship which they need instead of a supplier relationship is much greater than CRONOMANT's.

Our customers can be divided into three main groups:

A customers: approximately 60 These buy products mainly from product areas 1 and 2. They are interested almost exclusively in price, even though a growing number realize that they must manufacture products where the bought-in raw materials are of top quality and that they must use increasingly sophisticated raw materials in their production process.

CRONOMANT is much stronger in A customers in the Northeast and in large parts of Central USA. METAL is much stronger in A customers in Western USA and a little stronger in the South.

B customers: approximately 20 These buy products mainly from product areas 3 to 5. They demand high quality, wide range, first-class service, and a supplier who is a leader in applications and in R&D.

METAL is much stronger than CRONOMANT in the whole of the USA regarding B customers.

C customers: approximately 20 These buy products from the whole range, from the simplest to the most sophisticated. Their needs are the same as the B customers', but for areas 1 to 3 they often want two suppliers to avoid being overdependent on us.

Their strategy is to gain access to our high quality, first-class service, large range and our applications and R&D resources at the same time as they press down price levels on the simpler products by playing us off against CRONOMANT.

CRONOMANT is, above all, well in with the C customers in Northeastern and Central USA, where it sells product areas 1 to 3 on its low price levels. However, CRONOMANT also sells by presenting itself as a guarantee that we do not use our strong position to set our prices too high. 'CRONOMANT—THE alternative supplier' is their message.

4. Analysis of ourselves

The result of the discussion gave the following picture of our strengths and weaknesses:

Strengths	Weaknesses
<ul><li>Profitable, sound</li><li>Applications development</li><li>Company and product image</li><li>Two factories, both able to choose between two different production methods, giving great freedom to choose cheapest energy source</li><li>Large product range</li><li>Top quality</li><li>Marketing, organization</li><li>Delivery backup, dependability</li><li>Low production costs in product areas 3 to 5</li><li>Almost alone in Western USA and very strong in the South</li></ul>	<ul><li>Transport disadvantages in Northeastern region, most significant for product areas 1 and 2</li><li>Dependence on self-financing since not a member of a large group</li><li>Some customers want alternative supplier because of our dominant market position</li></ul>

'This looks really great,' exclaimed Wayne. 'And it's all the better because we are working to over 95 percent of capacity, which means that we spread fixed costs over optimal volume.'

'Doesn't CRONOMANT run competitor analyses?' said Spokane. 'Let's move on.'

5. Competitor analysis

This is the result of the discussion on CRONOMANT's strengths and weaknesses:

Strengths	Weaknesses
• Member of a large group with good solidity • Transport advantages in Northeast and also in parts of Central USA • Good company image in Northwest and parts of Central USA • Fairly good product image in product areas 1 to 3	• Low profitability, both for self and for group • Generally poor company image • Small R&D resources, at least 3 years behind us • Have no applications engineer worthy of the name • Only one production method, makes them dependent on price developments for certain energy sources • Poor quality in product areas 3 to 5 • Limited assortment in product areas 3 to 5 • Marketing amateurish; small, understaffed marketing organization

'Don't they do analyses of themselves?' asked Brando.

'I still don't understand why they're expanding their capacity. Do you?' said Spokane.

6. Comparison of forces

At company level: METAL vs. CRONOMANT
Geographical area: USA

Market success factors

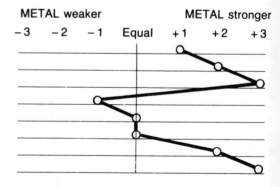

They continued making comparisons of forces for the different regions of the USA and for each product area. This is how one of CRONOMANT's strongest areas looked:

Product area: 1
Geographical area: North-East

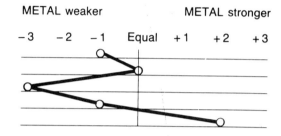

The picture fitted well with the view they had earlier. CRONOMANT was strong in the Northeast, particularly regarding simpler products where they were not handicapped by their relatively poorer service, deficiencies in marketing, product range, development and R&D resources.

In the same region, but for product area 3, the picture was like this:

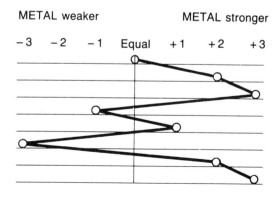

Since product area 3 includes significantly more sophisticated products than area 3, METAL has the overall competitive edge here even though CRONOMANT is fighting on its home market. Eight more comparisons of forces were made before it was decided that enough was enough.

'Now we've got a good idea of the situation,' said Spokane. He went up to the whiteboard and started to lecture: 'Now that we've worked through the first six steps in the BATTLE model, it's time to move on to step 7—CRONOMANT's options.'

Spokane then went through the theories concerning this step: 'There are three theories usually used for predicting what moves a competitor may make:

(1) Permanent routines
(2) Rational actors
(3) System characteristics

PERMANENT ROUTINES

The permanent routines theory says that if a person always goes the same way to work at exactly 8 o'clock every morning, always leaves punctually at 4.30 p.m., always goes past the newsstand on his way home, then he will continue to do so in the future.

Permanent routines theory is always used when making predictions, even if one is not always conscious of it. The theory often gives useful guidance, but must be applied with great caution since a skilled competitor is well aware of the danger of sticking to routines. One's appraisals must therefore be supplemented with the other theories, and one must be alert for tendencies that indicate that a competitor may be altering his routines.

RATIONAL ACTORS

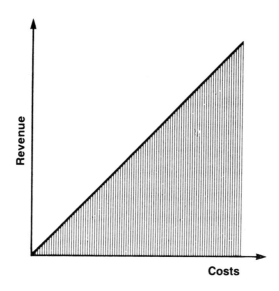

On the rational actors theory, a competitor's action is based on rational analyses. It is reasonable that the competitor acts in the way that is best for him. What the competitor considers profitable is what governs his activity in the market. If he is considering attack, then he most probably first balances expected revenue from the attack against expected costs.

Thus if one can establish what is profitable for a competitor, then one has an instrument for plotting his future activity. The problem is to be able to put oneself into his position and to map what is really rational from his point of view. He may, for example, take steps that appear irrational in the short term, but are rational in the long term.

Is the competitor rational anyway? He may be artistically inclined, governed by his feelings rather than by rational considerations, or he may be governed by a lust for power, or by prestige.

SYSTEM CHARACTERISTICS

The systems characteristics theory states that the opponent's system and routines contain given characteristics that cause him to act in a certain way. If these characteristics can be grasped, it is also possible to predict the opponent's future action. The problem is only that the

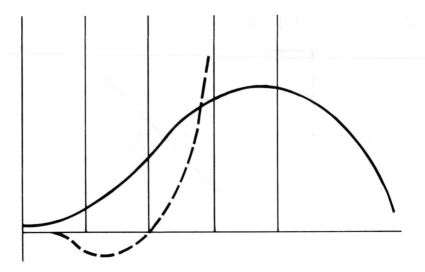

connections between system characteristics and how the competitor will act are usually very complex. The risk is therefore great that the simplified models we have discussed oversimplify reality.

In commercial life there are system characteristics that govern how to act 'just in time', the experience curve, the product life-cycle and portfolio matrices; and profitability models of the type of Bergman & Beving's R/RK can give good guidance as to how the competitor will act in a given situation.

If we know, for example, that our competitor is owned by Bergman & Beving, then we also know that his management is under heavy pressure as regards profitability and that it puts short-term profitability before increased market shares. If, on the other hand, the owner is a Japanese company, volume, market shares and growth are the top priorities and short-term profitability takes second place.

What we have to remember is that our competitors' options have to be assessed using the three theories *from his angle*, and not from ours.

Going through the first six stages of the BATTLE model has now given us our basic data.

In military life one generates two or more alternatives in which the opponent's various purposes, his main methods for achieving his purposes and the means (options) required for achieving them are noted down.

Then one notes down the opponent's greatest *weaknesses* for each alternative, what is most *dangerous* for us (both in the short term and

120

long term), what we think will most *probably* happen and what we think can happen at the *earliest*.

Napoleon said: 'The general must ask himself many times a day, "What do I do if the enemy attacks my front, my right, my left?" If he cannot answer this question, there is something wrong with his plan and he must quickly correct his mistake.'

'Okay,' said Spokane, 'I promise I won't lecture any more for a bit. Let's take time out for half an hour before we go any farther.'

During the break Nicklaus, who is an applications engineer, returned from a customer visit he had been unable to put off. Wayne and Spokane quickly filled him in on the problem, going through the stages of the BATTLE model that now festooned the walls. When the group had reassembled, they started to cross-examine Nicklaus to add the basic values hitherto lacking on CRONOMANT. As Spokane knew that the cross-examination would answer a lot of questions but also produce new ones, he had it recorded. After the meeting he and Wayne could go through the tape in peace and quiet and draw up an *intelligence plan* which would contain:

(1) Detailed *questions* (intelligence needs).
(2) Suitable *methods* for getting the answers.
(3) Suitable internal and external *sources*.
(4) The *person responsible* at METAL.
(5) A *time schedule* for collecting the information.

The chief responsibility for the intelligence plan became Wayne's, so that the work would be given highest priority.

'Why is CRONOMANT increasing production capacity by 60 percent when the market is only growing by 3 percent?' Spokane asked.

Nicklaus replied, 'They're not doing it all at once—in stages. In the first stage, they increase capacity by 30 percent. At the same time, they're preparing their plant for the next stage. The final decision on the next stage won't be taken for about another year. Then it'll be at least another year after that before they can use the new capacity.'

'Well,' said Wayne, 'That's something, anyway. So if we can only hold down their volume growth for a year, their board aren't going to be all that enthusiastic about decisions for more expansion. Where do they plan to place the increased volume?'

'They had several reasons for expanding capacity,' Nicklaus went on. 'First, they'd reached their ceiling. Then, they had to invest in new machines to manufacture the sophisticated products to acceptable quality. For another thing, their President got the market growth wrong. He thought the market would be growing by 5 to 6 percent a year, instead of 3 percent. And you know they're moving into Europe . . . ?'

'They're going to start selling in Europe?' Spokane ejaculated.

'Sure. Looks like it. I was golfing with their sales manager at the weekend. He talked as usual. They've opened a sales office in Germany—he's just got back. It looked like he was almost sorry afterwards, for telling me all this. He tried to make out he'd been on a conference in competition strategy, but that doesn't figure. They'd never get him to sit still a whole day.'

Castelo asked if it was true that their President was leaving.

'Fired,' Nicklaus answered laconically. 'Their new president's from IBM. Williams. He's been at IBM since he graduated from Stanford 18 years ago. Marketing director for their New York area.'

'Not good,' said Spokane. 'Now it'll be the whole IBM works all along the line. Their salesmen will become company heroes on commission, bonuses, incentive trips, every darned thing they can think of to get them to sell more. They'll go in for service, they'll go in for quality and applications and R&D, they'll have conferences and seminars. Here on in, a salesman and a couple of engineers will sit down with the customer and they'll make joint plans for customer development. But it's an ill wind. . . . Their costs will go up, so they should be interested in raising their prices.'

'Then we'll have to keep a firm grip on our salesmen and our applications engineers and the R&D people,' said Wayne. 'It takes at least a year before a new man can start doing any good, and a few more before you can say he knows his area. If they're going in for the IBM repertoire, they'll have to poach people from us. When does Williams start?'

Nicklaus knew the answer to this one. 'In a month. And he's not coming alone. He's bringing a sales manager with him from IBM and a group manager from the service side.'

'Does your sales manager friend say anything about where they plan to place all this new capacity?'

'Yes, it seems they're after the C customers. And since they are reckoning on significantly better quality, they can sell more from product area 3. Area 4 too.'

'What,' Castelo wanted to know, 'does the group say about CRONOMANT's invoice volume and profitability?'

'They seem most interested in holding the profitability level, increasing it if possible,' answered Nicklaus. 'They're definitely not going Japanese—building up market shares at the expense of short-term profitability.'

The discussion continued for a while. Wayne concluded the cross-examination by telling Nicklaus, 'Go on playing golf with their sales manager. It looks as if he's heading to be replaced by somebody with a little more IBM culture—and then he'll be even more talkative. Just see you don't tell him anything useful about us.'

Spokane summed up: 'We seem to have a good picture of CRONOMANT. Before we start making hypotheses about CRONOMANT's options, I'd like to rough out the battlefield where the marketing war will be fought and decided.' He stood up, went to the board and drew the following table:

CRONOMANT stronger	'Battlefield'	METAL stronger
NE USA A customers	NE USA B,C customers	Western USA A,B,C customers
Central USA A customers	Central USA B,C customers	Southern USA B customers
	Southern USA A,C customers	
	(EUROPE)	

'And, sure, we can attack the CRONOMANT A customers in the Northeast or in Central USA, but that would be like attacking a fortress where the walls are thickest and the cannons biggest. And of course they can attack our A,B,C customers in the West, or our B customers in the South, but then they're attacking us in terrain where we have all the advantages. Now everything seems to show that we're dealing with an opponent who can think rationally, so let us at this meeting today and tomorrow concentrate on the four "battlefield" boxes here. We can go through the other boxes later and see if we've overlooked anything. The two hypotheses regarding CRONOMANT's options were like this:'

Aim:	Volume increase • Get rapid compensation for capacity increase. Show that investment was correct.	Long-term profitability
Methods:	• Direct low-price drive to get volumes quickly. • Export EUROPE to place capacity. • Later marketing, service, quality, range, etc., drive.	• Marketing, service, quality, range, R&D, etc., drive. • Export EUROPE to place capacity. • Cautious price policy (hidden discounts).

- -

Options:		
	Lower price level	Hire: — Marketing staff — Salesmen — Applications engineers — R&D staff — Product engineers *from us*, from customers or elsewhere in the market
	Hidden discounts	
	Credit terms	
	Volume discounts	
		Conferences, seminars
	Export: Germany, England, France, Spain, Italy	Joint projects with customers
	Present oneself as 'the alternative supplier'	Free delivery

CRONOMANT's 'alternative 1: frontal attack'

The aim of the frontal attack is to create a rapid increase in volume to cover the investment in capacity. There is a desire to show the board that the decision to invest was correct, and to obtain a decision to carry out stage 2.

The attack opens with low price as a weapon. If this does not work, then hidden discounts are used to get orders. Free or heavily subsidized

124

delivery is offered as a way of attracting our A customers in the southern region. In Europe there is an attempt to 'dump' the largest possible quantities without actually being taken for 'dumping.' The lower the US price level, the easier it will be to sell cheaply in Europe without risking political intervention.

Present oneself as 'the alternative supplier', which C customers are known to appreciate since they wish to have two suppliers to choose between.

Step by step the marketing organization is built up; service and quality are improved, effort is put into applications development and the range is broadened. If these measures are successful, R&D is given priority so as to be able to compete in product areas 4 and 5.

Weaknesses of alternative 1
- On the southern and parts of the central USA battlefields the CRONOMANT image is rather poor. Probably not enough only to offer low prices
- Unknown in Europe
- Can the small marketing organization manage such a powerful offensive?
- Will deliveries be possible in view of running-up problems?
- Short-term profitability will dip. What will the group's management say?
- It is easy to start a price war but difficult to stop it. The risk is that only customers will benefit.

CRONOMANT's 'alternative 2: encirclement'

The aim of encirclement is to create long-term profitability. Key people are hired, in the first instance *from us* but also from customers and straight out of college, so as to increase resources for processing the market.

As far as ever possible with given staff resources, attempts are made to increase product range, raise quality, improve dependability of delivery, step up applications development and R&D.

Go in for conferences, seminars, establish partner relationships with customers. Avoid open price war, work through hidden discounts, credit terms and freight subsidies. In Europe, try to sell the largest possible volumes without risking counterattacks from European competitors or political measures as a result of excessively low prices.

Present oneself as a serious 'alternative supplier' who is trying hard to break METAL's lead to the benefit of free competition.

Weaknesses of alternative 2
- Does not tie up with group requirements on long-term profitability
- It takes a long time to build up marketing competence. There is a risk of never catching up unless there is real success in reducing *our* resources by hiring *our* staff
- It takes time before top management can be shown a result. First come the costs and only then the revenue
- Unknown firm in Europe.

Common to both alternatives
- Drive on European sales
- Positioning as 'the alternative supplier'
- Build-up of marketing organization
- Drive on quality, product range, service, applications development and R&D in the long run.

Most dangerous for METAL in the short term
- Price war as under alternative 1.

Most dangerous in the long term
- Build-up of marketing organization. Drive on quality, increased product range, service, applications development and R&D.

Most probable   If the outgoing President and Sales Manager decided, it would be alternative 1, 'frontal attack'.

With the IBM team now taking command, alternative 2, 'encirclement', is more probable.

What can happen at the earliest
- Appointment of key personnel (from us)
- Price war (hidden or open)
- European sales to a few customers in Germany.

The silence in the room was compact when the hypotheses were formulated and the meeting was clear what the worst-case consequences could be.

Spokane rose to his feet. He said, 'Tomorrow we're going to make plans for defeating the enemy. As I see it, we're going to wipe the floor with 'em.'

Wayne glanced at the others who looked surprised, almost depressed. Then he said, 'I hope we'll all be as certain as you are when we're through tomorrow. Some of us are thinking it looks rather tough. . . .'

Spokane interrupted. 'Of course I'm right. We're going to wipe the floor with them. See you 7 o'clock tomorrow morning.'

8 Our options

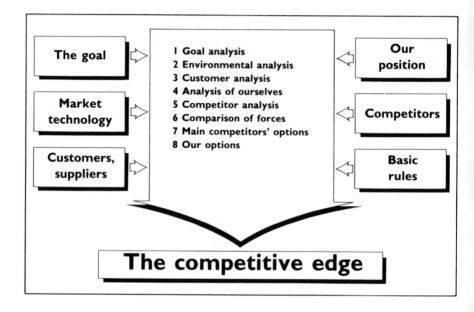

The goal → | 1 Goal analysis
2 Environmental analysis
3 Customer analysis
4 Analysis of ourselves
5 Competitor analysis
6 Comparison of forces
7 Main competitors' options
8 Our options | ← Our position

Market technology → | ← Competitors

Customers, suppliers → | ← Basic rules

The competitive edge

'So far,' said Spokane, 'we've been analyzing the situation. Now finally it's time for us to make our battle plan for dealing with the CRONOMANT attack we know is on the way. Before we start, let's go through the basic military rules on how to win a war. These basic rules have grown out of experience in war. They are generally valid and they work regardless of what strategic principles are applied. They run like this:

(1) Set a goal and stick to it.
(2) Maintain good morale.
(3) Act aggressively.
(4) Aim for surprise.
(5) Concentrate forces.
(6) Make sure your own forces are secure.

(7) Use your forces economically.
(8) Coordinate.
(9) Try to be adaptable.
(10) Strive for simplicity.

'What do you think?' asked Spokane.

'If it worked for Julius Caesar, for Alexander the Great, for Napoleon and General Patton, then it's good enough for us, too,' said Wayne. 'My father was with Patton in North Africa and Europe. I remember when he told us about Patton's speech to the troops before the start of the August offensive in Avranches in 1944:

"Remember, I don't want any reports about 'I'm holding my position'. We ain't holding anything. Let the Krauts do that. We're going to advance all the time, not sit and hold anything. Yes, contact with the enemy. Hold him hard and beat the life out of him. Our plan of operations is to advance and go on advancing over, under or right through the enemy. We have only one motto: 'Audacious, audacious, always audacious.' Remember that. Whether we win or die, 'Always audacious'."'

'But we can also learn something from Liddell Hart's studies of military history,' added Castelo. 'He showed that it was mainly indirect methods that were decisive in 274 out of 280 battles. In only six cases was it the direct method—the one Patton preferred—that won the day. Patton won because of his enormous superiority.'

'What are we waiting for,' said Ewing. 'They think they can up their capacity, take market shares, pinch our customers and start selling sophisticated products. Let's show them who they're up against.'

Spokane went up to the board. 'Let's go back to yesterday morning when we went through "goal analysis." We formulated our aim as retaining our present market share of 70 percent in a market that is growing by 3 percent a year, while keeping high profitability—wasn't that it?'

'Right,' said Wayne. 'But we also agreed the goal was probably unrealistic.'

'Then our short-term goal, that is for the next year, could be to get CRONOMANT to shelve the decision on further expansion of capacity,' said Castelo.

'And we can do that by making sure they have such lousy capacity utilization that the question becomes hypothetical,' added Ewing.

'Are we agreed, then,' Wayne interposed, 'that our short-term goal is to give up market shares voluntarily, but not to such an extent that they start thinking about increasing their capacity any further? Our short-term profitability will have to adapt to this overall goal. Longer term, and I mean over the next three-year period, we maintain our high level of profitability.'

Everybody nodded to show their understanding and agreement.

'Now we're agreed on the revised goal, we can go on to decide what other views we have,' said Spokane.

Wayne went to the board and summarized the result of the discussion:

METAL's criteria for choosing options:
  (1) Achieve the goal.
  (2) Continue stress on wide product range and quality.
  (3) Keep the large market shares for sophisticated products.
  (4) Work for total-economic good solutions for customers— become partners with the customer.
  (5) Encourage CRONOMANT sales to Europe to unload the pressure on the US market.
  (6) Exploit CRONOMANT's weaknesses—strike from our own strength.
  (7) Act aggressively—strike first.
  (8) Keep our R&D lead.

It was now Spokane's turn at the board: 'While we're considering our options, there are some things we have to do that don't depend on which alternative we choose. We write down the steps that are common to the various alternatives—then we can see exactly what the alternatives look like.'

The result of the discussion that followed was like this:

Measures common to the different alternatives
  (1) Development discussions immediately with all key personnel whom CRONOMANT might think of bringing over to them. Offer all employees options that can be cashed in two years when we go public. Make salary adjustments where necessary, plus extra bonuses for orders taken within the next four months, to bind customers to us before the CRONOMANT offensive gets under way.
  (2) Intensification of customer visits, above all to those within the defined 'battlefield.'
  (3) Price adjustments. Lower prices on competition-sensitive products and raise them on nonsensitive products (IBM

strategy). Volume discounts to increase customer credibility among B and C customers.

(4) We should state, and show in action, that we are as interested as the customer himself in his development. We are partners with the customer, not suppliers.

(5) Encourage CRONOMANT to export to Europe.

(6) Check out our capacity status so that we do not suddenly have delivery problems due to changes in product mix. Examine possibilities of increasing capacity by 10 percent with small investment of resources, preferably through shift rescheduling or similar measures.

(7) Drive on active intelligence service.

The two agreed alternatives for action were as follows.

Our alternative 1: 'the iron glove'

(1) Creation of a B range for a number of volume products in areas 1 to 3, priced very low.

(2) Selective hidden discounts, advantageous credit terms, subsidized freight for important deals.

(3) Differentiated service levels. Basic service free, but all other service supplied at extra charge.

(4) Cooperate with European competitors with the main purpose of helping them break into CRONOMANT's customer base in Northeastern USA. A form of 'stab-in-the-back' tactic.

(5) Offer very advantageous prices to CRONOMANT's main stronghold, i.e. the A customers in Northeastern and Central USA, thus forcing on them price cuts that only affect themselves: we are not affected since we sell next to nothing to these customers. A very aggressive action since we thereby extend the 'battlefield.'

Is this alternative a suitable one? Mmmm. . . . If absolutely necessary for reaching the short-term goal—yes. But it goes against the whole of our company ethos.

Perhaps too aggressive. There is a risk that their group management feel they are losing face and react emotionally.

Is the alternative feasible? Yes, given an immediate decision.

Will the alternative lead to the desired goal? Yes, the short-term goal, but to the long-term goal—doubtful. It is easy to start a price war, but often considerably more difficult to stop it.

Our alternative 2: 'coexistence' (on our terms)

(1) Recruitment of key people (chiefly from among CRONOMANT's best customers) so as to be able to give our customers even better service, applications development, quality and product range.

(2) Setting up *Applications Centers* at our two factories, where we show different applications with our products included as raw materials, plus advice to customers on how they can develop further.

(3) Setting up an *Applications Team* to go the rounds of customers and together plan how they can increase their competitiveness by using our most sophisticated products as raw materials in their manufacturing processes. We help customers with development of their market and processes.

(4) Establishment of *Training Centers* at which we train customers' personnel in knowledge of materials, production control and the 'just-in-time' concept. Training Centers would be staffed by external specialists, with our own specialists and salesmen working there alternately.

(5) Intensive drive on Research and Development. Sales of know-how, patents and knowledge of production processes to European competitors, to keep our development costs down, but also to be able, if our supplies should be interrupted, to offer our customers deliveries from alternative suppliers. Sales to Europe through our partners' sales organizations, but not to kill CRONOMANT's European sales since we want them to export there.

(6) Drive on conferences, fairs, articles in trade press, information sheets.

(7) Increased drive on raising quality, level of service and developing product range in consultation with our customers.

Is the alternative suitable? Yes, definitely.

Is the alternative feasible? Yes, but it requires very complex efforts on the part of the organization. An immediate decision is necessary and large staff and financial resources are required.

132

Will this alternative lead to the goal? Yes, given quick action. Highest tempo necessary. Measures common to both alternatives are absolutely necessary for goal achievement.

'Before we go any further,' said Spokane, 'let's just check that the two alternatives are formulated correctly. A table of relevant alternatives is marked by the fact that:

- The alternatives lead to our goal
- The alternatives are comparable
- The range of conceivable strategies is covered
- Two or more alternatives cannot be put into practice simultaneously.

'What do you think?' Spokane asked.

'Well, we can go into detail on how well the alternatives agree with the formulated demands, but I think we have produced two clear main options. Either we become simple price-warriors or else we go in for being sophisticated marketeers,' said Wayne.

'I think in fact the alternatives are three,' said Ewing. 'The common measures for the different alternatives could also be an alternative by themselves.'

'Brilliant, eh?' said Wayne.

Agreement was total. The mood was euphoric. Only the war-paint and the war-dance were lacking for the whole thing to have been taken from a cowboy-'n-injuns film.

Spokane broke the silence. 'So we have decided on three alternatives. One—the "iron glove," two—"coexistence" and three—what I'll call the "middle way." The "middle way" is also included in the other alternatives. Shall we go further in the BATTLE model?'

9 *Comparison of alternatives*

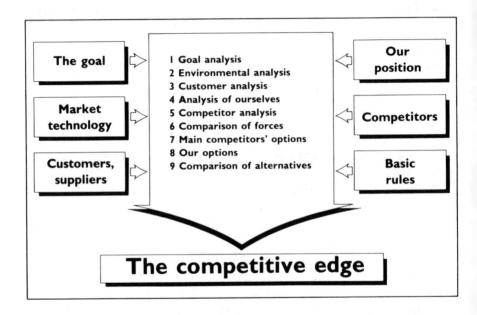

The goal		1 Goal analysis		Our position

Spokane introduced this part of the seminar with a little brushing up of theory: 'Now we're finally ready to compare CRONOMANT's various options with our own. We can do this with an exercise which is usually called "confrontation" in the army. What we do in fact is a small "course-of-the-war" study where we try to predict the result of each confrontation between one of the opponent's options and one of our own.

'When we appraise the result of each confrontation it is important that we start with the evaluation criteria we produced earlier when we were going through our various options. To gain a clear view in confrontation and reduce the risk of anything being left out on the way, it may be a good idea to use a matrix in which we describe in words, from our point of view, the outcome of the various confrontations.

Our option \ Enemy option	1	2
1 Goal evaluation	Value judgment	Value judgment
2 Goal evaluation	Value judgment	Value judgment
3 Goal evaluation	Value judgment	Value judgment

I. The iron glove versus the frontal attack

'One thing is clear—the price war will be bloody. Profitability will be nonexistent for a long time to come,' was Castelo's comment.

'Yes, and sooner or later we'll have to bargain with CRONOMANT to get profitability up again,' said Wayne.

'And customers who've been able to buy cheap will do anything so they can play us off against each other to get the price war going all over again,' added Brando.

Ewing said, 'The measures that are common to each alternative are in fact aggressive enough, but the aggression in this alternative— there's just no sense in it.'

'Right,' Wayne agreed. 'Sure, we'd achieve the short-term goal, but the long-term goal can go and . . . .'

Spokane asked, 'How does the outcome of this confrontation fit in with your assessments?'

'It definitely ties up with our "Act aggressively—strike first,"' answered Brando. 'But it'll be hard to manage our long-term orientation to better service, to higher quality, to the customer-adapted product range, partnership relations with customers, applications development, plus the Research and Development drive. We can't handle a price war *and* our long-term orientation. We must choose—we can't do both.'

135

Spokane's next question was, 'What do you consider Patton would have thought about this particular confrontation?'

Castelo replied. 'He'd definitely have liked our "iron glove" option. But we mustn't forget when we compare ourselves with Patton that he nearly always fought from a position of enormous superiority.'

Wayne, who understood what Spokane was getting at, concluded, 'Even Patton would realize that you don't use price as a weapon against an enemy who has price as his strongest card. Especially as our opponent has big financial guns to back him up, which he's sure ready to use if we challenge his group management's prestige.'

II. The iron glove versus encirclement

Ewing introduced this one: 'This looks like an improbable confrontation. We behave hyper-aggressively on the market while the people who are always ready to fight on prices suddenly leave us with a walk-over and build up their resources for processing the market instead.'

Brando noted, 'If we fight them with "iron glove," they'd soon be forced to give up their "encirclement" option and go in for their "frontal attack" instead.'

'And what's more,' Castelo said, 'presumably we would soon be in big trouble deliverywise because we would get a lot of orders for the unprofitable products from areas 1 and 2. This just doesn't figure with our drive on sophisticated products.'

Wayne defined this: 'So that in practice this alternative is the same as the first one, with the difference that we would sell too many of the unprofitable products. In this way, we'd be up against delivery problems that would also affect the customers who depend on our reliability here.'

III. Coexistence versus frontal attack

Brando was enthusiastic. 'This is a confrontation I like. They go on fighting with price as a weapon and we work with the market trend towards greater demands on service and development of more and more sophisticated products. But I'm afraid,' he went on, 'there's a risk they could expand their capacity utilization too much, which means we don't achieve our short-term goal and stop them from developing. Apart from that, the situation matches our earlier appraisals fairly well.'

Ewing agreed. 'There's a serious risk they'll be all too successful at selling out their overproduction. And then there's another risk, that they'll decide to expand their capacity some more in about a year.'

Castelo wondered. 'Question is, whether we can manage our magnificent market-processing drive if they decide on a price war.'

'No,' said Wayne. 'We'll probably have to do this in stages. Decide about each stage after we've done a thorough analysis of how well we're maintaining our shares of the market.'

'Right. If we go for "coexistence" and they go to war on prices, we'll probably have to shift strategy—at least partly. "Coexistence" is no-go if they choose "frontal attack."' This was Spokane again.

'It's not so likely their new management will choose "frontal attack" unless they get the idea that we're making price war on them,' said Wayne.

'Well,' said Ewing, 'there's some customers would sure be glad to give them that idea. But couldn't Nicklaus talk a little about where we stand, when he plays golf with their sales manager. That's what politicians do, like when they want to test a new tax proposal. They leak the proposal via some journalist; they get a reaction. If the reaction isn't too violent, they go ahead.'

'An excellent suggestion,' said Spokane. 'As far as I know, it's entirely legal, too. No risk that we'll be examined by the antitrust people or whoever, thinking we're trying some kind of competition limitation.'

IV. Coexistence versus encirclement

Castelo said, 'Now it's something like! This confrontation seems to be the ideal one—we achieve all our goals and our assessments. Their IBM management can work the way they're used to, and their profitability and ours will be fine, both short-term and long-term.'

Ewing agreed. 'Yes, this looks fine. But don't forget that when we analyzed this before, we thought their "encirclement" was *the worst threat* for us in the long run.'

'If we only keep the pace up and don't lose anybody to them, I consider we can beat their "encirclement,"' Wayne considered.

Spokane said, 'If their new management could increase their capacity utilization by exporting to Europe and take a bit of our market in product areas 1 and 2 without us hitting back on prices, then encirclement is probably the line they'd take. The customers aren't going to like us and CRONOMANT fighting in this way. They'll do various things to set us against CRONOMANT good and proper, so they can get lower prices.'

'This confrontation looks good,' Wayne said. 'But it's not enough for us to send Nicklaus to talk out of turn when he meets the CRONOMANT sales manager on the golf course. Anyway, we didn't think he was going to last as long as this with their IBM team. No, the tactic for how we leak what we intend to do is something I'd like to work out myself. What we can be satisfied with now is to say we have to make it clear to CRONOMANT's management what we want and how we intend to go about it, so they don't start off a price war based on poor intelligence from some customer, or from some trigger-happy salesman who wants an order at all costs. Just look at the superpowers, how they inspect each other's maneuvers to be sure there's no hanky-panky going on.'

V. The middle way versus frontal attack

Ewing introduced this comparison. 'There's a clear risk that they will take over-large market shares in this confrontation, if we are not prepared to use a lot of dirty tricks from "iron glove." We really have to be very careful about following rigid price policies and so on—we have to work very flexibly. We have to be prepared to stretch one or two of our assessments if we're to reach our short-term goal.'

Castelo: 'But a situation like that is a darned sight easier to handle than if we were to choose to fight with "iron glove" or the "coexistence" option against their "frontal attack." '

Brando said, 'Right, that figures. If they choose "frontal attack" as their strategy, then "middle way" has got to be our best main strategy.'

'It looks like it,' Wayne agreed. 'My appreciation is that the middle way option favors both our goals and assessments if CRONOMANT decides to attack us frontally.'

Spokane concurred. 'That's so. "Middle way" laced with a few dirty tricks from "iron glove" would presumably work for us very well against their "frontal attack." '

VI. The middle way versus encirclement

'As long as we keep our personnel,' said Wayne, 'this confrontation is tough for them. I consider we definitely achieve our short-term goal. But if they're too successful in building up a market processing capability, we can have problems reaching our long-term goal and fulfilling our basic assessments.'

Brando saw it in the same way. 'I guess we have to be a little more aggressive than what "middle way" says, if we're not to lose our lead in "market processing."'

Ewing interposed, 'But how well we do on "middle way" depends almost entirely on how well they do with their "encirclement." What we need is for our intelligence service to get reliable and continual information on how successful they are at building up their market processing capability. If they aren't particularly successful, we keep our lead by settling for "middle way" and going on as we usually do.'

'Right,' said Spokane. '"Middle way" works if they are not too successful with their "encirclement." But if they are, then we can have serious problems ahead.'

10 Choice of strategy

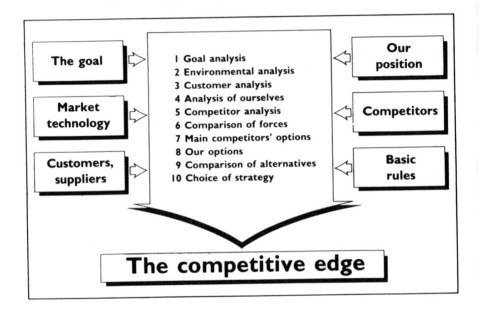

The goal	⇨	1 Goal analysis	⇦	Our position
Market technology	⇨	2 Environmental analysis 3 Customer analysis 4 Analysis of ourselves 5 Competitor analysis 6 Comparison of forces 7 Main competitors' options	⇦	Competitors
Customers, suppliers	⇨	8 Our options 9 Comparison of alternatives 10 Choice of strategy	⇦	Basic rules

The competitive edge

'I think we should decide immediately to carry out all the measures that are common for the three options, that is the "middle way,"' said Spokane. '"Middle way" is the best we can do in the present situation until we know more about what strategy CRONOMANT are going to choose and what market tactics they're going to use for carrying out that strategy.'

Wayne said, 'This sounds fine. Now we only have to make sure our intelligence service functions and gives us reliable information about what CRONOMANT are doing, so we won't be caught with our pants down while we're working out the details of our own market operation.'

'Sure,' Spokane agreed. 'If our intelligence doesn't function we're in for big problems, whether or not we manage to come to some "understanding" with CRONOMANT.'

'What do you others think?' Wayne asked.

Brando thought 'middle way' was a really great alternative. 'And also we should put time and resources into building up an effective intelligence service to find out what alternative CRONOMANT chooses.'

Ewing nodded. 'Now I agree entirely with Spokane when he said yesterday evening that we'd wipe the floor with CRONOMANT. We will—as long as we continue to work as systematically as we're doing here. But we must be on our guard now they've got such competent management.'

'But,' Castelo objected, 'what if the new management go all the way with their "frontal attack," or if CRONOMANT carries out the whole of its "encirclement"? Shouldn't we work out right now what our response should be?'

'I'm glad you raised that,' Spokane said. 'We've settled for "middle way" because we don't really believe CRONOMANT will really implement "frontal attack"—or "encirclement"—all the way. We think they'll do something in between, but nearer "encirclement." But if they run either option flat out, then it's a great advantage if we have a detailed plan ready for how to counter them. What I propose we do now is to plan "middle way" in detail. Then we work in two groups to make detailed plans for countering their two extreme options. As I see it, we can take a whole lot of ideas from the alternatives we've roughed out ourselves.'

Wayne: 'Right. Let's get going.'

And so we leave Spokane, Wayne, Brando, Ewing, Nicklaus and Castelo now that they have worked through the ten steps of the BATTLE model.

The case study is based on an authentic case which Lieutenant-Colonel Kaj Wahlberg and I worked on, but Sandvik Coromant was not involved. It didn't happen in the USA, the persons had other names and the competitor's new management didn't come over from IBM. Otherwise, most of it is true.

SOME CONCLUDING VIEWS

What I have spent ten chapters describing is how to win the market struggle. When I am working with large companies, the disposition of their strategy plans differs from the ten steps of the BATTLE model. A company's disposition might be like this:

(1) Summary
(2) Internal factors
   - Business idea
   - Earlier development (by function)
   - Present situation (by function)
   - Strengths, weaknesses
(3) External factors
   - Market developments
   - Technical developments
   - Competitors
   - Threats, opportunities
(4) Goals
(5) Strategy and programs of action
   - Products and product development
   - Marketing
   - Production
   - Diversification and acquisition
   - Organization
(6) Resource requirements
   - Personnel
   - Investments
   - Projecting, development, production
   - Sales resources
(7) Expected results
   - Market shares
   - Order flow
   - Invoicing
   - Result/profitability
(8) Implementation
   - Action
   - Time schedule
   - Responsibility
(9) Follow-up
   - Responsibility
   - Point in time

There is no contradiction between this disposition and the BATTLE model. The BATTLE model represents the process of producing the strategic plan. The result is then presented following the group's own guidelines. So it is not a matter of either/or, but of both.

It is my hope that this book can contribute to a more competitive spirit within commercial life, when companies start to work more systematically, and in teams, through their competition strategies and tactical plans, and build up functioning intelligence services.

Good luck in the Marketing War!

Group tasks for the competitive edge

The group tasks from which you can choose for analyzing your strategic situation and then making decisions that will give you the competitive edge are gathered here at the end of the book.

My purpose in this was that you should first read the book and then use a teamwork approach to the tasks you find relevant for your own company's specific situation. I recommend that members of strategy seminars read through the book twice before the seminar starts, and that the leader of the seminar prepares carefully by obtaining the documentation necessary for answering problems arising during the group work.

The seminar result will naturally be more satisfactory if the leader has already worked with BATTLE for a long period, but this is no requirement for using the model.

The time horizon the strategy plan is to cover depends on the industry or sector. It is often five years in the largest commercial groups, and this then applies to all group units. My own view is that the strategy plan should cover a 'reasonable' horizon, but there is nothing to prevent you extending the plan at future seminars to cover a further period.

1. GOAL ANALYSIS

Group task 1:1

Thomas Watson Sr was of the opinion that the main reason for IBM's great successes has been the fundamental values he formulated in 1924.

1. What are your company's fundamental values?
2. How do you now ensure that they are lived up to through practical action?
3. What can you do to ensure that they are lived up to better?

Group task 1:2

Describe the business idea(s) for the area you are responsible for. If more ideas are needed, produce them.

A business idea should answer the following questions:

1. What are your markets? Who are your customers?
2. What *customer needs* do you fulfill?
3. What is your *offer* to the market?
4. Why should the customer choose you and not a competitor? What is *unique* and *superior* about your offer to the customer?

Group task 1:3

1. What *qualitative* goals have you? For example:
   - Technological leadership
   - Market leadership
   - Best-priced/performanced supplier
   - Best service
   - Leadership in quality
2. What *quantitative* goals have you? For example:
   - Growth
   - Relative market share
   - Yield on tied-up capital
   - Capital turnover rate
   - Invoicing volume
   - Turnover/employee
3. Time factor: When will the goals be reached? Sub-goals?
4. Present position: What is the present position regarding each goal?
5. Do you experience these goals as realistic?

2. ENVIRONMENTAL ANALYSIS

Group task 2:1

1. In what market segment are you working:
   - What geographical area?
   - What products?
   - What markets/customers?

Market / Product				

2. Fill in the matrix with what you consider important. For example:
   - Market size
   - Market growth
   - Market share
   - Profitability
   - Own invoicing

Group task 2:2

The product life-cycle curve
1. In what phase of the life-cycle curve is/are the market/markets in which you are working?
2. Fill in your main products on the life-cycle curve.

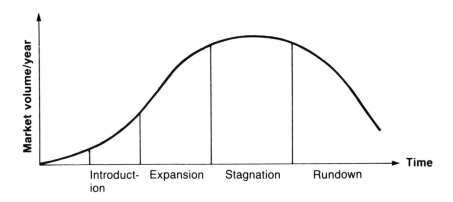

3. Where will your products be in x years, if no special steps are taken?
4. What steps are needed to achieve a good balance between old and new products?
5. Where are the technologies you employ today on the S-curve just now?
6. Can you make a technological flank attack on your competitors by changing technology?

Group task 2:3

The BCG model
1. What is the growth rate in the market segments you process?
2. What is your position (i.e. relative market share) in relation to your largest competitor in this market?

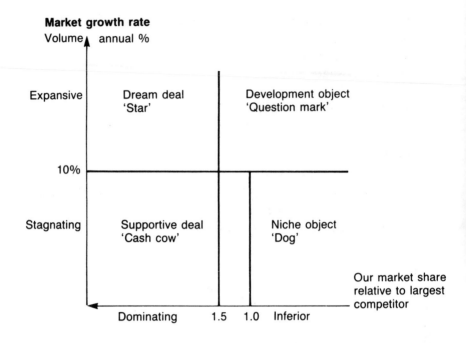

Market growth rate
Volume ▲ annual %

Expansive	Dream deal 'Star'	Development object 'Question mark'
10%		
Stagnating	Supportive deal 'Cash cow'	Niche object 'Dog'

Our market share relative to largest competitor

Dominating   1.5   1.0   Inferior

3. Fill in your position on the BCG model regarding the various market segments you process.

   Use a large circle to show that the deal produces a large part of company invoicing and a small one to show the opposite. Try to make the various circles proportional to the part of company invoicing they represent.

4. What are your conclusions from your placing in the BCG model?

Group task 2:4

The GE model

1. Decide what factors make a market attractive from the point of view of your total operation.

2. Rank the factors (most important first) and then 'weight' them. A total weight of 1.00 should be distributed among the various factors.

3. Decide what factors determine your competitiveness in the markets you currently operate in, or those you wish to enter.

4. See point 2.

5. Give points to the different operations included in your total operation. Use a reasonable number of operations (3 to 6)—no

fancy work. The model is meant for making a rough assessment of operations.

6. Calculate weight × points regarding market attractiveness for the various operations. Calculate weight × points regarding competitiveness for the various operations.
7. Insert the various operations in the GE model
Large circle = larger market.
Small circle = small market.
Own market share = 'pie slice' proportional to market size.
8. What conclusions do you draw from your placing of the different operations in the GE model?
9. Can you alter your placing in the GE model by taking steps that improve the points scoring?
10. What steps do you suggest?
11. What would the different steps cost?
12. How is your placing in the GE model altered by the suggested steps?

Group task 2:5

Positioning in the market (alternative 1)
1. Study how Volvo's Private Cars Division, or ACO's, market is described using the positioning diagrams in Chapter 2, Environmental analysis
2. What do you think should be put on the *x* axis or the *y* axis for your own market or markets? You may need to draw several positioning diagrams before you find the one that is 'right.'
3. Where do you and your competitors come in the positioning diagram?
4. In what direction is the market developing?
5. What conclusions do you draw from the market development?
6. What are your conclusions from your own and your competitors' positions on the diagram?

Group task 2:6

Positioning in the market (alternative 2) Two positioning variables were chosen for the Volvo and ACO positioning diagram. It can often be an advantage to work with four positioning variables, as in the case of the study association in Chapter 2.

1. Write down a number of positioning variables.
2. If you have more than four, try and group some of them as in the case of the study association in Chapter 2
3. Draw in your position for the four positioning variables, equidistant from the origin.
4. Draw in your competitors' positions relative to your own.
5. In what direction is the market developing?
6. What conclusions do you draw from the market development?
7. What are your conclusions from your own and your competitors' positions in the diagram?

Group task 2:7

Threat/opportunity analysis
Geographical area: _____
Market/product: _____

Opportunity to be grasped

	Opportunities	Suggested action
• Market		
• Technology		
• Social/political development		
• Other		

Threat to be overcome

	Threat	Suggested action
• Market		
• Technology		
• Social/political development		
• Other		

3. CUSTOMER ANALYSIS

Group task 3:1

What do your various customer groups *really* buy?

1. For the largest customer groups (2 to 4 groups), what are the most important *purchasing factors*?
2. Rank the different purchasing factors, most important first, for each customer group.

Bear in mind that if you sell through middlemen, it is important to distinguish what each link buys. The retailer, for example, buys:

- A good product
- A good net margin
- Good marketing
- Secure deliveries
- Good service.

However, the final customer buys:

- Flexibility
- Design
- Security package
- Features
- Ease of use.

If you sell mainframe computers to a company, then perhaps the company's management buys:

- Image
- Security
- Future development capacity
- Price/performance
- Independence of supplier.

However, the final customer buys:

- Applications
- Ease of use
- Possibility of switching programs between different computers
- Service
- Upgradability.

Group task 3:2

How do you reinforce your customers' dependence on you? How do you select customers?

Some factors that increase your negotiating strength *vis-à-vis* your customers:

1. The customer buys only small quantities from you in relation to your total sales.
2. The customer lacks a qualified alternative supplier.
3. It takes the customer a great deal of time and expense to find an alternative supplier.
4. There is a small risk that the customer decides to produce the product/service himself.
5. The customer incurs large changeover costs if he switches to another supplier.

Some factors that counter price pressure from customers:

1. The customer's costs for your product/service are a small part of his total purchase costs.
2. High quality demands from customer. Quality faults costly for customer.
3. Your product saves much money for the customer.
4. Tailormade product/service.
5. The customer's operation is profitable and he can fairly easily pass on high purchase costs to *his* customers.

(SOURCE: Freely adapted from *Competitive Strategy*, M. Porter, Free Press)

Group task 3:3

How do you strengthen your negotiating position *vis-à-vis* suppliers? How do you select suppliers?

Some factors that increase your negotiating strength *vis-à-vis* suppliers:

1. You have several suppliers, or can easily get alternative suppliers.
2. You are an important customer for your supplier. The supplier is anxious to use you as a reference.
3. You avoid collaboration with a supplier who makes it difficult or expensive for you to change suppliers (e.g. tailormade solutions).

4. You encourage the emergence of alternative suppliers.
5. You try to use standardized products.
6. Possibility of manufacturing the product/service yourself.

(SOURCE: Freely adapted from *Competitive Strategy*, M. Porter, Free Press)

4. ANALYSIS OF OURSELVES

Group task 4:1

The experience curve   The logic of the BCG model is based on the fact that the unit cost of a product or service sinks over time if one can go on producing and selling it for a period. This is because one buys larger volumes, improves methods, routines and the production process, designs cheaper solutions, selects more rational means of distribution, and so on.

As a result of learning, economy of scale, design modifications and changes of technology, the cost of a more or less standardized product or service sinks by 20–30 percent per doubling of cumulative volume.

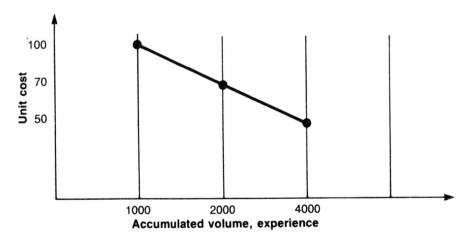

The experience curve fulfills all the conditions for being idealized, and it is therefore important to consider whether one accepts the main line of thought. If one does, two conclusions can be drawn:

153

1. Growth markets are the most interesting, for here it is possible to move more rapidly down the curve.
2. A large share of the market is more interesting than a small one, for here one can move down the curve more rapidly than one's competitors.

There are four bases for the experience effect:

1. *Learning.* Personal learning, group learning, cooperation between groups or units.
2. *Economies of scale.* Larger quantity of units manufactured = larger denominator to divide by. However, economy of scale is not only about manufacturing. It also concerns purchasing, distribution, service, R&D, etc.
3. *Design.* With time and number of units manufactured, designs and production methods are improved, and cheaper materials are selected.
4. *Technology.* Increased technological inputs such as mechanization, robots, computer control, more electronics in the products, change of electronics.

Work task
1. Choose a unit for analysis (e.g. the company, a business area). Scoring from 0 to 3, note in the appropriate box the probable 'experience effect,' i.e. lowering of cost per unit that you have at the moment owing to your present volumes and your efforts so far to benefit from the 'experience effect.'
2. Can you improve your position on the curve?
3. In which boxes, and by how much?
4. How do you do this?
5. What action should be taken?

Cost reduction appears in the following functions	Cost reduction		
	Learning	Scale economy	Designs Production methods Material changes Technological changes
Purchase			
R&D			
Production			
Distribution			
Sales			
Administration			
Other			

Group task 4:2

1. Study the positioning diagram from the environmental analysis.
2. What conclusions do you draw from your own and your competitors' positions in the diagram?
3. What steps do you suggest?

Group task 4:3

Strength/weakness analysis
Geographical area: _____
Market/product: _____

Strength to build on

	Strength	Suggested action
● Marketing		
● R&D		
● Production		
● Materials administration		
● Personnel		
● Finance		
● Administration		

Weakness to overcome

	Weaknesses	Suggested action
● Marketing		
● R&D		
● Production		
● Materials administration		
● Personnel		
● Finance		
● Administration		

5. COMPETITOR ANALYSIS

Group task 5:1

1. Who are your competitors?
2. Who is/are your main competitor(s)?
3. Who owns the competition?
4. What are the owner's goals for the operation?
5. If the competitor is a subsidiary of a larger group, what are the goals of the subsidiary's management?

6. Get the positioning diagram from the environmental analysis. How do you think the competitor views his own market positioning?
7. How does the competitor view threats/possibilities in his surroundings?

SUPPLEMENTARY TABLE A

Threat/opportunity analysis   Competitor: _____
Geographical area: _____
Market/product: _____

Opportunity to be grasped

	What opportunities?	*Expected action*
• Market	_____	_____
• Technology	_____	_____
• Social/political development	_____	_____
• Other	_____	_____
	_____	_____
	_____	_____
	_____	_____
	_____	_____

Threat to be overcome

	Threat	*Expected action*
• Market	_____	_____
• Technology	_____	_____
• Social/political development	_____	_____
• Other	_____	_____
	_____	_____
	_____	_____
	_____	_____
	_____	_____

157

SUPPLEMENTARY TABLE B

Strength/weakness analysis   Competitor: _____
Geographical area: _____
Market/product: _____

Strength to build on

	Strength	Expected action
● Marketing	_____	_____
● R&D	_____	_____
● Production	_____	_____
● Materials administration	_____	_____
● Personnel	_____	_____
● Finance	_____	_____
● Administration	_____	_____
	_____	_____
	_____	_____
	_____	_____

Weakness to improve

	.Weakness	Expected action
● Marketing	_____	_____
● R&D	_____	_____
● Production	_____	_____
● Materials administration	_____	_____
● Personnel	_____	_____
● Finance	_____	_____
● Administration	_____	_____
	_____	_____
	_____	_____
	_____	_____

Group task 5:2

Draw up an intelligence plan
1. Work out detailed *questions* (intelligence needs).
2. Suitable *method* of finding the answers.
3. State suitable internal and external *sources*.
4. State our person *responsible*.
5. Make a *time schedule* for collection of information.

6. COMPARISON OF FORCES

Group task 6:1

1. In the market in which you are competing, what are the market success factors?
2. Rank the success factors, with the most important first.
3. How do you presently stand in relation to 'your competitor'?
4. What does the future position look like?
5. What environmental changes affect this picture?
6. What action do you expect of 'your competitor'?
7. What action have you taken?
8. What are your conclusions?

Note You may need to draw several strength comparisons, both at the overall level and for different market segments. Study the Spendrup example from the introductory chapter in this book for guidance. Note, too, that Spendrup was forced to concentrate on a sub-segment of the market (Premium Beer and the Stockholm area) to be able to compete successfully with Pripps, since Pripps was thirteen times larger than Spendrup.

Do you also have to concentrate on a sub-segment, or can you succeed by improving your position in the present market segment?

7. MAIN COMPETITORS' OPTIONS

Group task 7:1

Take out your information from the earlier competitor analysis. Add to the analysis with the three theories used for predicting what the competitor may possibly do:

1. The permanent routines
2. The rational actors
3. System characteristics.

Make two or three hypotheses regarding the competitor's options:

1. What different purposes can the competitor have?

2. What different methods can he use to achieve his purposes?
3. What different opportunities can he exploit?

Group task 7:2

1. Formulate the various hypotheses.
2. What weaknesses are there in the different alternatives?
3. What is common to the different alternatives?
4. What differentiates the alternatives?
5. What is the worst threat in the short term?
6. What is the worst threat in the long term?
7. What is most probable?
8. What can happen at the earliest?

8. OUR OPTIONS

Group task 8:1

1. What goals and assessments do you have?
2. What alternatives do you have?
   If you wish, you can use the same approach as the one used earlier to plot the main competitors' options:

   - Purpose
   - Methods
   - Opportunities
3. Common action regardless of alternative.

4. Check whether each alternative:

   - Is appropriate?
   - Is feasible?
   - Leads to the goal?

9. COMPARISON OF ALTERNATIVES

Group task 9:1

1. Confront each of the competitor's alternatives with each of our own according to this pattern:

Our option ＼ Enemy	1	2
1 Goal evaluation	Value judgment	Value judgment
2 Goal evaluation	Value judgment	Value judgment
3 Goal evaluation	Value judgment	Value judgment

2. How well does each confrontation fulfill our goals and assessments?

10. CHOICE OF STRATEGY

Group task 10:1

1. What strategy have you chosen?
2. Why?
3. Plan the strategy in detail:

   - Measures
   - Resources
   - Responsibility
   - Time schedule.